CURSES, PLAGUES, AND PANDEMONIUM

Finding Peace, Provision and Protection in Perilous Times

Holly Lewerenz

CURSES, PLAGUES, AND PANDEMONIUM: Finding Peace, Provision and Protection in Perilous Times
by Holly Lewerenz

Published by:
On Time Writing
"Publications for Such a Time as This"
P.O. Box 87765
Carol Stream, IL 60188

Cover Design and Typesetting:
Susan Harring

Dedication

I would like to dedicate this book to all of humanity, who along with myself, feel trapped in a chaotic, uncertain world in which we face a daily deluge of problems—health, family, job, business, finances, relationships—you name it!

Though it may seem like there are no lasting solutions, I assure you that there is One. His Name is Jesus. All solutions and blessings come from knowing Him. I honor Jesus as my Savior, Lord, Deliverer, Healer, Provider and Protector.

It's time to stop going around that mountain of struggle and impossibility one more time and go with me into an exciting journey of freedom—freedom from juggling a continuous stream of problems—into the victorious life Christ promised to give to us.

> The thief does not come except to steal, and to kill, and to destroy. I have come that they may have life, and that they may have it more abundantly. (John 10:10)

Table of Contents

Foreword

Holly Lewerenz has masterfully woven together an incredible narrative on the vital importance of being prepared and trusting God as our Only Source in these uncertain times against the backdrop of economic and political upheaval, natural disasters, and the division, hatred and ideologies that threaten America and the world. *Curses, Plagues, and Pandemonium: Finding Peace, Provision and Protection in Perilous Times* should be a mainstay of every believer, who is seeking the power of a supernatural, loving God to heal, deliver, protect, and provide for their needs as well as those who may be questioning the existence and identity of God, His plan for their life in the "here and now," and where they will spend eternity.

This timely book addresses the fear and frustration that arises from trying to cope with the sometimes overwhelming challenges of daily life. Through sound biblical principles, personal miracle stories, and a prophetic perspective, the author offers hope and powerful keys for overcoming those problems that seem to be unsolvable. It's time for you to experience freedom once and for all from everything that has held you back. Walk in victory, and receive all the good promises of God that Christ has purchased for you!

—Greg Mauro
Vice President of Ministries, Morris Cerullo World Evangelism
Author of *The Blessing of Serving Another Man's Ministry*
facebook.com/TheBlessingOfServingAnotherMansMinistry

Endorsements

Curses, Plagues, and Pandemonium is an exceptional teaching tool—a veritable classroom manual on recovery. Everyone roots for an underdog and cheers when they win. This insightful writing is sure to bring light to the dark and painful areas of our lives and cause joy to subjugate depression. Having known Holly now for nearly two decades, I can attest to the fact that in addition to the accurate handling of scriptural texts and her excellent moral character, she has captured the mastery of simplicity and clarity in communicating hope to the hopeless...healing to the broken. *Curses, Plagues, and Pandemonium* is a must-read for everyone who has felt small and alone. Say goodbye to discouragement and hello to a new kind of living. My highest recommendation for *Curses, Plagues, and Pandemonium*.

—Rev. David R. Wilkinson
Pastor, Freedom Church at the Lake (Lake of the Ozarks)
Ghostwriter/Editor at DRW Publishing House
drwpublishinghouse@gmail.com

I just finished reading the book, *Curses, Plagues, and Pandemonium: Finding Peace, Provision and Protection in Perilous Times*. Holly Lewerenz has assimilated a lot of scriptures and personal knowledge into the book. I was especially impressed by her words, "Faith cannot be simply intellectual assent. Faith has to be real, alive, and birthed out of our heart. The Bible shows us how."

And, my favorite sentence is, "The Word of God has to fill our heart to produce the faith that brings results "'for out of the abundance of our heart the mouth speaketh.'" (Matthew 12:34) Another favorite of mine is: "Peace will remove confusion, keep you on the right path, and prevent you from making mistakes." I feel these sentences of wisdom are what people desire and need.

I also like the fact that in the special feature at the back of the book, the author addresses the subject of the baptism with the Holy Spirit with breadth and depth. I like what she had to say on the subject because she stays positive and doesn't let "tongues" become a divisive matter of first-class and second-class Christians.

In *Curses, Plagues, and Pandemonium*, the author not only shows us how to be freed from the curses of our lives but also how to have a healthy Christian lifestyle that Jesus called the abundant life.

—Rev. Dr. Bill Calvin
Associate Pastor, Bloomingdale Church
Professor at Christian Life College
bloomingdalechurch.org

Holly Lewerenz' skill sets of writing and composition are very superior! This offering of *Curses, Plagues, and Pandemonium: Finding Peace, Provision and Protection in Perilous Times* is not only top-notch, but I believe it will also nurture those who read it. Holly has keen insight into the subject matter she is writing about and has done the necessary and painstaking research to make sure that this book is complete, literal, and understandable to her readers.

I highly recommend Holly's book, *Curses, Plagues, and Pandemonium: Finding Peace, Provision and Protection in Perilous Times* as a must-read if you want to be set free from the attacks of the enemy and achieve victory in your daily walk with the Lord!

—Dr. Robert E. Houston
Sr. Pastor, Mercy Seat MB Church
Author of *See You in the Morning*
roberthouston.org

Holly gives some great insights into the ministry of deliverance. As a deliverance minister myself, I was intrigued when I read this manuscript at some of her thoughts. This book is full of great knowledge and practical application for the reader. If you want to be set free or set people free this resource is a powerful tool.

—Kathy DeGraw
Founder and Author
Kathy DeGraw Ministries
www.kathydegrawministries.org
Unshackled and *Discerning and Destroying the Works of Satan*

Introduction

Witchcraft, generational, territorial and other types of curses are all very real. We hear about curses in the Bible, especially in the Old Testament. In chapters 2 and 3 of this book, I reveal the origin of the curse and the specific curses that the people of Israel suffered as a nation and individually because they rebelled against God. These curses still apply to the human race today.

One very relevant example of the manifestation of a modern-day curse is seen in the coronavirus plague (covid-19) that is terrorizing the world at the time of the writing of this book. Plagues are prophesied in Matthew 24 and the book of Revelation as well as in other scriptures of the Bible. These passages certainly foretell and aptly describe what is happening in the world today.

There are accounts in the Bible of sorcerers, witches and others, who practiced the occult and put curses upon individuals or groups of people. Examples are the sorcerers of Egypt that stood in Pharaoh's court, or those in the kingdoms of Babylon, or the Medes and Persians, where Daniel was carried off into captivity. God turned the circumstances in his favor and mightily used Daniel to influence those nations. In the book of Acts, we read about a girl, who was a fortune teller, as well as a devious man, Elymas the sorcerer, who tried to prevent Paul from sharing the gospel with the governor of the island of Paphos.

Jesus came to set people free from the curse—all those

who would believe He is the Son of God. "Christ purchased our freedom [redeeming us] from the curse (doom) of the Law [and its condemnation] by [Himself] becoming a curse for us, for it is written [in the Scriptures], Cursed is everyone who hangs on a tree (is crucified);" (Galatians 3:13 AMPC)

If you are born again, then you are no longer under the curse of the law of sin and death. You have been redeemed into the kingdom of God. As a citizen of the kingdom of God, your portion is the blessing of the Lord. In chapter 4, you will discover the blessings that are yours in Christ.

As you can see on the evening news, our world is changing. Darkness, evil and ungodliness exist everywhere. We need to have an understanding of how to get free from the enemy's attacks that wage an aggressive assault against us and our loved ones. In this book, you will learn how God supernaturally intervenes in the lives of His people to set them free and to bring His plans and purposes to pass in the earth.

You may already believe that God can heal, deliver, provide and protect. Praise God! Many Christians believe this, too, and have experienced His blessing in their health, family, finances, relationships, job or in some other area of their life—only to come back to the same situation they were in before—within a few days, months or years.

Why is this? Jesus paid the price for our freedom; yet, while we are still on this sin-cursed earth, there will be spiritual battles. Witchcraft and generational curses may wreak havoc in your family and in your life…demonic attacks and oppression will try to gain entry to your mind, emotions and health…the forces of darkness and evil will try to subvert God's plans and purposes for your life.

This book will teach you how to be delivered from the deception, influence and control of Satan and his demonic hordes as they strive to infiltrate your life, your family, and your environment—and how to maintain the victory Jesus purchased for you!

Chapter 1

Murphy's Law: Feeling Overwhelmed

You've heard of, and probably even acknowledged its presence in your own circumstances more than once, a phenomenon commonly called "Murphy's law," or in other words, "if something can go wrong it will."

Most of us from time to time get that feeling of being overwhelmed. Someone may say, "Now what? What else can go wrong with this project?" Or maybe, "Not again! I just got over the flu; why am I sick again?"

Life's problems, some tiny, some terrible, seem to come at the worst time. After you've been high on the mountain rejoicing over a victory or joyful event in your life, POW—you plunge into the valley of despair as yet another problem hits you and turns your world upside down.

I'm here to tell you there's hope. God's promises are for you. Keep reading and discover how to access these wonderful blessings that await you and your loved ones.

Do Curses Really Exist in Today's Modern World?

There are lots of different opinions about curses…from laughing at the thought of being cursed to being sure that someone has put a witchcraft spell on you.

What do you think about when you picture the word "curse"…A man spewing out foul language? A witch conjuring up a smoldering cauldron of weird ingredients guaranteed to zap its intended victim? A cackling, old woman with a creepy face and gruesome voice casting a wicked spell on a Disney princess? Or, just a seemingly ordinary string of upsetting events or bad things happening to you or those you love?

You see curses and their disastrous effects in fairy tales and horror stories alike, in video games, and even in the "how-to" instructions you can look up online if you're really mad at someone and want to get even. Most of us don't take this variety of curses too seriously or plan to invoke them ourselves.

A Curse Cannot Come that Has No Cause

However, curses are very real and can affect your life if you don't recognize them for what they are and know how to combat them effectively. The book of Proverbs in the Bible has something interesting to say about curses. Let's look at this in several different translations (bolded emphasis mine):

The *King James Version* of Proverbs 26:2 says,

As the bird by wandering, as the swallow by flying, so the curse **causeless** shall not come.

The *Amplified Bible* expands a little on its meaning,

> Like the sparrow in her wandering, like the swallow in her flying, So the curse without cause does not come and alight [**on the undeserving**].

And, *The Passion Translation* gives yet another perspective,

> An undeserved curse will be **powerless to harm** you. It may flutter over you like a bird, but it will find no place to land.

The Message translation says it like this,

> You have as **little to fear** from an undeserved curse as from the dart of a wren or the swoop of a swallow.

And finally, the *New Life Version* adds yet another dimension,

> Like a sparrow in its traveling, like a swallow in its flying, so **bad words said against someone** without reason do not come to rest.

Notice the words I've emphasized in bold type: The first two translations show clearly that curses don't come without a reason. There is a "root" behind the curse—whether spiritual or natural—that gives the curse permission to operate in a person's life.

The next two translations encourage us that we are not helpless against random curses striking us or our family. But, rather they are "powerless to harm us" and we have "little to fear" if there's nothing in our lives that has invited them in.

Speak Blessing, Not Cursing

The *New Life Version* describes a curse as "bad words said against someone." This definition shows that our words are extremely important, whether good or bad. We can speak blessings or curses upon another. "Death and life are in the power of the tongue: and they that love it shall eat the fruit thereof" (Proverbs 18:21). Or in other words, "Words kill, words give life; they're either poison or fruit—you choose" (MSG).

God gave the Israelites a mandate, found in Deuteronomy 30:19, to reject the curse. This same choice faces you and me today. Notice, the choice you make even affects your family.

> I call heaven and earth as witnesses today against you, that I have set before you life and death, blessing and cursing; therefore choose life, that both you and your descendants may live;

"You're Too Skinny!"

I grew up in an average, middle-class home. From the time I was a small child, my parents tried everything to get me to eat. "A bird eats more than you do," they'd tell me in exasperation. "You're too skinny." (Nobody ever heard of "body shaming" back then.) As I went on through my childhood, teens and even into adulthood, I developed a bad self-image. I thought, "I'll never get a date. The guys all think I'm too skinny."

Later on, I found out God loved me just as I was and that I was beautiful in His sight (just like you are, dear reader). This helped somewhat, but I still shied away from people, having become introverted and convinced that somehow something was wrong with me. As I grew in Christ, my poor self-image was replaced with a "God-image." Those earlier hurts I suffered were healed. (And, I'm not skinny or shy anymore either!)

My parents didn't mean to set in motion that self-conscious self-image I had for years to come. They were just concerned about my health. However, I want to caution parents, and anybody else as well, about the importance of building up your children or others with your words, not tearing them down.

Sticks and Stones

Do you remember the old adage, "Sticks and stones may break my bones, but words will never hurt me."? As kids, we were quick to repeat that saying to defend ourselves when someone spoke mean words to us. It's a lie—Words do hurt! The story I just told you about seemingly innocent words spoken from a heart that only wanted to help shows how our simple comments can have a long-lasting effect on someone else. In essence, we put a curse on someone when we speak negatively about them, even sometimes when we laugh and assure them, "I was just joking."

One component of "New Age" philosophy (more about this in chapter 9) is to "chant" words that speak what you want to come about. In the Church we make "faith confessions" of what we are believing God for. What's the difference? It's in the source and the focus that is behind the words. The New Age chants are empowered by the devil and their focus is man's self-actualization without God. The source of a Christian's words is the Holy Spirit and the focus is (or should be) Christ-centered.

In either case, words are powerful and in them lie the seed, through faith, to bring about what is desired. With our words, we either bless or curse a person, a situation or even other living things. There have been incidents where sick livestock have improved or a wilted plant has suddenly come alive after positive words were spoken over the cattle or the rosebush. The apostle Paul warned, "Speak blessing, not cursing, over those who reject and persecute you" (Romans 12:14 TPT). The story that follows demonstrates the victory that can come from a positive faith confession.

An Unpopular Stand of Faith

"But, what should I do?" I asked my friend as I sobbed almost uncontrollably in the church lobby. "The pastor says I have to go to the doctor before they will pray for me anymore." Let's back up a bit to where the story begins. I'd been leaning over a stair railing in my house, stretching to reach a hanging plant with my watering can. The plant fell and slammed my arm against the railing. Immediately, my arm turned black and blue, swelled up like a balloon, and hurt unbearably. You could physically feel where the breaks in the bones occurred and see the dislocation caused by them.

Now I believe in God's power to heal, so I immediately called friends to pray. I started confessing God's Word that I am "healed by the stripes of Jesus" along with multiple other healing scriptures. No immediate change, but I kept speaking "blessing" not "cursing" over my arm despite the fact I could hardly stand the pain. Fast forward...

The next Sunday I went to church and asked one of the pastors to pray. He did, but then fearing that gangrene was developing, he said, "Your arm is turning green; you need to see a doctor right away. I'm not going to pray any more until you get medical help." I was so upset I started to cry. This is where I ran into my friend, who attended the same church. "What should I do?" I asked, "I want to obey church leadership, but I don't want to go to a doctor. I believe I'm already healed by the stripes of Jesus."

Long story short, I stuck with my faith confession despite how the situation looked in the natural, and within a few short weeks (not months as it would have taken in a cast), my arm was totally healed—glory to God—all bruising and swelling gone, bones whole and in place, strong, and I've never had any problems with my arm since. *(NOTE: I am not advising anyone not to go to a doctor or get medical help unless you know that you know that you know you've heard the voice of the Lord telling you otherwise. People can have faith that God will work through their doctor and his prescribed treatment, too.)*

Who or What Is Influencing You?

In addition to our words, there's another influence we sometimes overlook. It's what our eyes see and our ears hear. Some kids (and adults, too) love to watch horror movies or violent crime dramas on TV. "It's only make believe," they explain. Pornography is on the rise; many movies and video games are violent, sexually immoral and filled with profanity. All these things open the door to the devil—and everything he brings: curses, sickness, poverty, strife, anger, fear, danger and harm.

Even watching too much news with its barrage of hatred, division, terror, devastating natural disasters or other frightening reports, to say nothing about the ungodly opinions that are voiced, can desensitize our emotions or cause anger and fear to rise up in us. However, in this day in which we live, it is necessary and wise to keep up with what's going on in the world because many current events are lining up with Bible prophecy. We cannot afford to be deceived or asleep…It's time to watch and pray!

Choose those with whom you spend your time wisely. God has put us in the middle of a corrupt world where we are to be light and influence others for Christ, not the other way around. We must be careful that we're not becoming like those around us that do not know Christ, or joining in on activities that don't honor God. Ask yourself, "If Jesus were here, would He want me to be here, say this, or do that?"

I don't want to sound legalistic—We are free in Christ, but as the apostle Paul put it, "It's true that our freedom allows us to do anything, but that doesn't mean that everything we do is good for us. I'm free to do as I choose, but I choose to never be enslaved to anything" (1 Corinthians 6:12 TPT).

If you've allowed an open door to the devil through your words, sin or ungodly focus, activities or associations, you can close it right now. Just repent and accept God's forgiveness! "If we confess our sins, He is faithful and just to forgive us our sins and to cleanse us from all unrighteousness" (1 John 1:9 NKJV).

It's Time for a Change

Are you feeling overwhelmed? Are you experiencing an overflow of problems or disappointments?

It's time to stop going around that mountain (of despair and defeat) one more time and claim your freedom from the continuous stream of problems flowing into your life. Enter into the victorious promises of God and the glorious destiny He has planned for you.

Key Points

- Many people are stuck in a defeated or victim mentality.
- Curses are real-life attacks that affect us and our families.
- Don't let the circumstances or problems of life overwhelm you.
- You can experience freedom from every curse!
- You can choose life or death, blessing or cursing.

Action Assignment:
Ask the Holy Spirit to reveal to you areas in your life where you have felt "stuck" and unable to get free or solve the issues that hold you back. Write down what He reveals to you. (Starting a journal or notebook to keep your insights in while you're reading this book would be a great help toward freedom and reaching your God-given destiny.)

Chapter 2

The Curse Enters the Earth

You might be wondering, "Ok, so where did these curses come from and how can I get rid of them?" First things first, let's discover the origin of curses. God's Word, the Bible, plainly reveals how it all started.

In the beginning God created the heavens and the earth. The earth was without form, and void; and darkness was on the face of the deep. And the Spirit of God was hovering over the face of the waters. Then God said, "Let there be light"; and there was light. And God saw the light, that **it was good**; and God divided the light from the darkness. God called the light Day, and the darkness He called Night. So the evening and the morning were the first day. (Genesis 1:1–5 NKJV – emphasis mine)

In the beginning, God created the heavens and the earth. In the same manner He created light, God went on to divide the waters and create land; then the Bible says He created trees and vegetation, the sun, moon and stars, and filled the air with birds, the seas with fish, and the land with every kind of animal. As in the scripture above, God proclaimed over all His wonderful creation, "It is good." His work not yet complete, God, in all His majestic genius, created His masterpiece: man!

> So God created man in His own image; in the image of God He created him; male and female He created them. Then **God blessed them**, and God said to them, "Be fruitful and multiply; fill the earth and subdue it; have dominion over the fish of the sea, over the birds of the air, and over every living thing that moves on the earth." ... Then **God saw everything that He had made, and indeed it was very good**... (Genesis 1:27–28, 31 NKJV – emphasis mine)

Once again, God said it was very good. Notice too, He blessed them! God blessed all that He had created—everything on the earth and in the heavens—all that He had made was good. No sign of any curse anywhere!

An important point needs to be made here...How did God create everything? With His words! The Bible also points out, "Then God said, "Let Us make man in Our image, according to Our likeness..." (verse 26).

Remember, in chapter 1, we said that words are extremely important. They are the tools for creating, and since we are made in God's image, we have been given the ability to create with our words, too. Later on, we'll find out that our words not only have the ability to create, but they have the ability to curse others or to allow curses into our own lives.

A Little Bit of Heaven on Earth

You probably remember the story of how God created the magnificent, lush garden of Eden with its own flowing river for watering the Garden. Let's pick up the story here,

> Then the LORD God took the man and put him in the garden of Eden to tend and keep it. And the LORD God commanded the man, saying, "Of every tree of the garden you may freely eat; but of the tree of the knowledge of good and evil you shall not eat, for in the day that you eat of it **you shall surely die**" (Genesis 2:15–17 NKJV – emphasis mine).

Adam and Eve were given dominion over all that was in the earth including the Garden. There were beautiful trees and plants filled with luscious fruit and herbs—everything they could ever want was at their fingertips. God gave them only one instruction they had to follow… they could not eat of the tree of the knowledge of good and evil. Sounds pretty easy, doesn't it, when they had so many others to choose from?

Fear and Shame Enter the Human Race

Enter from stage left (or maybe right, we don't really know, of course), the villain, Satan, here known as "the serpent." Our story proceeds, filled with intrigue and suspense, and the plot thickens...

4 Then the serpent said to the woman, "**You will not surely die.**

5 For God knows that in the day you eat of it your eyes will be opened, and you will be like God, knowing good and evil."

6 So when the woman saw that the tree was good for food, that it was pleasant to the eyes, and a tree desirable to make one wise, she took of its fruit and ate. She also gave to her husband with her, and he ate.

7 Then the eyes of both of them were opened, and they knew that they were naked; and they sewed fig leaves together and made themselves coverings.

8 And they heard the sound of the LORD God walking in the garden in the cool of the day, and Adam and his wife hid themselves from the presence of the LORD God among the trees of the garden.

9 Then the LORD God called to Adam and said to him, "Where are you?"

10 So he said, "I heard Your voice in the garden, and **I was afraid** because I was naked; and I hid myself."

[11] And He said, "Who told you that you were naked? Have you eaten from the tree of which I commanded you that you should not eat?"
[12] Then the man said, "The woman whom You gave to be with me, she gave me of the tree, and I ate."
[13] And the LORD God said to the woman, "What is this you have done?"
The woman said, "**The serpent deceived me**, and I ate."
(Genesis 3:4–13 NKJV – emphasis mine)

The Curse Enters the Earth

This one encounter changed the course of history forever. This one act of rebellion, of man's disobedience to the instructions of a holy, sovereign God, brought fear, and then the curse, into Adam and Eve's lives and the lives of their descendants, all men, women and children who would ever populate the earth.

[14] So the LORD God said to the serpent:
"Because you have done this,
You are cursed more than all cattle,
And more than every beast of the field;
On your belly you shall go,
And you shall eat dust
All the days of your life.
[15] And I will put enmity
Between you and the woman,

And between your seed and her Seed;
He shall bruise your head,
And you shall bruise His heel."
¹⁶ To the woman He said:
**"I will greatly multiply your sorrow and
your conception;**
In pain you shall bring forth children;
Your desire shall be for your husband,
And he shall rule over you."
¹⁷ Then to Adam He said, **"Because you
have heeded the voice of your wife,
and have eaten from the tree of which I
commanded you, saying, 'You shall not
eat of it':**
"Cursed is the ground for your sake;
In toil you shall eat of it
All the days of your life.
¹⁸ Both thorns and thistles it shall bring
forth for you,
And you shall eat the herb of the field.
¹⁹ In the sweat of your face you shall eat
bread
Till you return to the ground,
For out of it you were taken;
For dust you are,
And to dust you shall return."
(Genesis 3:14–19 NKJV – emphasis mine)

Notice how fear entered into man's heart (verse 10).
Then, God systematically pronounced the curse (caused

by sin and man's rebellion, not God's will or desire) on the serpent (Satan) in verses 14–15, on the woman (Eve) in verse 16, and on the man (Adam) in verses 17–19 for each of their parts in the fall from glory.

When the curse was pronounced on the devil and on man, it was not a one-time event. Later came the Old Testament Law of God, and because no man could keep this law, this became the "curse of the law of sin and death" (Romans 8:2). Every child is born with this "sin nature" before they are even old enough to talk or walk or commit any actual act of sin. Sin is now inherent in the human species. But, God provided a way out through Jesus (more about that later)!

Financial Curses

One of the areas that "Murphy's Law" or biblically speaking, "the curse" seems to be most active in is our finances. In the book of Haggai, God had called His people to build the Temple, but they were complacent, ignoring the command of God through His prophet Haggai, who spoke this rebuke,

> "This is what the LORD of Heaven's Armies says: The people are saying, 'The time has not yet come to rebuild the house of the LORD.'" Then the LORD sent this message through the prophet Haggai: "Why are you living in luxurious houses while my house lies in ruins? This is what the LORD of Heaven's Armies says: Look

at what's happening to you! **You have planted much but harvest little.** You eat but are not satisfied. You drink but are still thirsty. You put on clothes but cannot keep warm. **Your wages disappear as though you were putting them in pockets filled with holes!** "This is what the LORD of Heaven's Armies says: Look at what's happening to you! Now go up into the hills, bring down timber, and **rebuild my house.** Then I will take pleasure in it and be honored, says the LORD. **You hoped for rich harvests, but they were poor. And when you brought your harvest home, I blew it away.** Why? Because my house lies in ruins, says the LORD of Heaven's Armies, while all of you are busy building your own fine houses. It's because of you that the heavens withhold the dew and the earth produces no crops. I have called for a drought on your fields and hills—a drought to wither the grain and grapes and olive trees and all your other crops, **a drought to starve you and your livestock and to ruin everything you have worked so hard to get.**" Then Zerubbabel son of Shealtiel, and Jeshua son of Jehozadak, the high priest, and the whole remnant of God's people began to obey the message from the LORD their God. When they heard the words of

the prophet Haggai, whom the LORD their
God had sent, the people feared the LORD.
Then Haggai, the LORD's messenger, gave
the people this message from the LORD:
"I am with you, says the LORD!" (Haggai
1:2–13 NLT – emphasis mine)

Notice how important God's house is to Him; in this
text, His house is the Temple. Today, for believers, it is
the Church. The nation of Israel, in their self-centered and
materially-focused lack of devotion to the Lord's house
suffered great loss. But, when they got back on track with
the right priorities and began putting God, and His Temple,
first, He lifted the curse and began to bless them again. "I
am with you, says the Lord!"

Look at this well-known scripture:

You are under a curse, for your whole
nation has been cheating me. Bring all the
tithes into the storehouse so there will be
enough food in my Temple. If you do,"
says the LORD of Heaven's Armies, "I will
open the windows of heaven for you. I will
pour out a blessing so great you won't have
enough room to take it in! Try it! Put me to
the test! (Malachi 3:9–10 NLT – emphasis
mine)

The principle of "tithing is controversial among many
in the Church. Some say it's Old Testament, so believers

are free from it; others say tithing existed before the law, so it's for everybody. My own personal opinion is that as believers in Jesus Christ, we are not bound by law to tithe. However, why would you not want to do it freely and to honor God?

Look at the blessing that comes from tithing: "I will open the windows of heaven for you. I will pour out a blessing so great you won't have enough room to take it in!" and in the *King James Version*, the next verse, verse 11, says, "And I will rebuke the devourer for your sakes..." Who is the devourer? That's Satan, his demons, sickness, loss...anything that diminishes or steals from you, "The thief cometh not, but for to steal, and to kill, and to destroy..." (John 10:10). That's the best insurance policy I've ever seen—when we tithe, God will make sure we, our family, and our possessions are safe.

A man I know, I believe is the victim of a financial curse. He is smart, creative and resourceful, but no matter how hard he works, he cannot seem to succeed at any job he undertakes. He earns money, but it just slips away and he winds up broke and in debt. He'll get a new idea or try a proven success strategy, but something always happens, an accident or injury, or an unexpected expense or loss pops up to put an end to any temporary gain he experiences. Is this just "bad luck" or lack of effort or ability on his part? I don't believe so.

Look at this scripture with me: "Beloved, I pray that in every way you may succeed and prosper and be in good health [physically], just as [I know] your soul prospers [spiritually]" (3 John 2 AMP). Do you see something here? God's will is prosperity, but He is a God of divine order. First, the soul must prosper, then our finances and health will follow.

The man in this story says he believes in Jesus...but there is no outward evidence. He doesn't attend church, He doesn't tithe or give to the poor. Of course, it is by grace we are saved, and not by works, but if we truly have a relationship with Jesus, not just an intellectual belief in Him, we will have a love for the Church and God's people. We will want to give to God's work and help others.

There are principles in the Word of God that govern our Christian experience and the blessings we receive from God. Ignoring or rebelling against these principles God has set forth for our benefit will result in forfeiting His blessings, or worse—opening the door to a curse or attack of the enemy.

More about how to get rid of financial curses later, but for now, let's look further at what God's Word says about the Church, which is the body of Christ. We need each other, even more so now than ever, as we navigate our way through the last days before Christ's return.

The Community of Believers

The Bible instructs, "Let us not neglect our church meetings, as some people do, but encourage and warn each other, especially now that the day of his coming back again is drawing near." (Hebrews 10:25 TLB). I have found in my own personal experience that when I'm faithful in attending and serving in my local church, things go much better for me. God's blessings abound, and I can always trust that His protection and provision will be there for my family and me.

I thank God for His Church. I remember one of my earliest healing experiences that also greatly affected my finances. I had injured my back at work, and the doctors discovered that the discs on my spine had degenerated. It was a mess...Off work for three months, I laid flat on my back, much of the time on the hard floor because that seemed to be least painful. I could barely move without excruciating pain! The doctor suggested possible surgery but wasn't very optimistic about the outcome.

I was a new Christian and had just heard about God's divine healing power, so I hobbled slowly over to the church which was located just a couple doors from the apartment building where I lived. The pastor and his assistant prayed for me and anointed me with oil as described in the book of James. Wow! The pain instantly disappeared! I literally ran home rejoicing. I bent over, swung my arms up and around, and jumped up and down. No pain, no stiffness...I was completely healed! I went back to the doctor. He agreed that it had to be a miracle and said I needed no further treatment. To God be the glory!

We can be a Christian and commune with the Lord all by ourselves. But, how much more effective and encouraging it is to share Him with others of like-minded faith. We need our church family, and I praise God for mine!

Key Points

- God created all things, and afterward He said, "It is good."
- God gave man dominion over every living thing.
- The devil deceived Eve into doing what God had prohibited.
- When man disobeyed God, it brought a curse on the earth.
- The Church is a place of blessing and encouragement.

Action Assignment:

Write down in your journal or notebook one or more things you've said or done (or failed to say or do) that you know are in disobedience to the Word of God. Think about it... What were the results of what you said or did (or failed to say or do)? Read 1 John 1:9. Then, from your heart, repent and ask God to forgive you and cleanse you from all unrighteousness (guilt, sin and its results) and bring restoration to you, others, and the situation.

Chapter 3

An Inventory of Curses

Deuteronomy, chapter 28, lists both the blessings and curses that resulted because of man's fall in the Garden. In the next chapter, we'll get to the blessings, but for now, let's take a look at all the horrifying consequences of the curse of disobedience that entered into the earth.

The list of curses in Deuteronomy shows the seriousness with which we need to obey God and the severity of the results of disobedience. **It's true, in the New Covenant, we have been set free from the curse of the law through Jesus' sacrifice on the cross,** but God still calls us to obey His instructions, so that we may receive the benefits and rewards that come with obedience. With curses and plagues like these, it's easy to see how much we need Jesus…and how great and awesome His salvation really is—not only for eternal life, but for life here on earth, too.

Though we are free from the curse through Jesus Christ, if we open the door even a crack and allow the devil access, he will try to put the curse back on us. This is why we need to know and recognize what is in the curse and when it is Satan that is behind the attacks and troubles you and I may be facing, so that we can know how to appropriate what Christ did on the cross to break every curse.

> [15] "But if you refuse to listen to the LORD your God and do not obey all the commands and decrees I am giving you today, all these curses will come and overwhelm you:
> [16] Your towns and your fields will be cursed.
> [17] Your fruit baskets and breadboards will be cursed.
> [18] Your children and your crops will be cursed.
> The offspring of your herds and flocks will be cursed.
> [19] Wherever you go and whatever you do, you will be cursed.
> [20] "The LORD himself will send on you curses, confusion, and frustration in everything you do, until at last you are completely destroyed for doing evil and abandoning me.
> [21] The LORD will afflict you with diseases until none of you are left in the land you are about to enter and occupy.
> [22] The LORD will strike you with wasting diseases, fever, and inflammation, with scorching heat and drought, and with blight

and mildew. These disasters will pursue you until you die.

²³ The skies above will be as unyielding as bronze, and the earth beneath will be as hard as iron.

²⁴ The LORD will change the rain that falls on your land into powder, and dust will pour down from the sky until you are destroyed.

²⁵ "The LORD will cause you to be defeated by your enemies. You will attack your enemies from one direction, but you will scatter from them in seven! You will be an object of horror to all the kingdoms of the earth.

²⁶ Your corpses will be food for all the scavenging birds and wild animals, and no one will be there to chase them away.

²⁷ "The LORD will afflict you with the boils of Egypt and with tumors, scurvy, and the itch, from which you cannot be cured.

²⁸ The LORD will strike you with madness, blindness, and panic.

²⁹ You will grope around in broad daylight like a blind person groping in the darkness, but you will not find your way. You will be oppressed and robbed continually, and no one will come to save you.

³⁰ "You will be engaged to a woman, but another man will sleep with her. You will

build a house, but someone else will live in it. You will plant a vineyard, but you will never enjoy its fruit.

³¹ Your ox will be butchered before your eyes, but you will not eat a single bite of the meat. Your donkey will be taken from you, never to be returned. Your sheep and goats will be given to your enemies, and no one will be there to help you.

³² You will watch as your sons and daughters are taken away as slaves. Your heart will break for them, but you won't be able to help them.

³³ A foreign nation you have never heard about will eat the crops you worked so hard to grow. You will suffer under constant oppression and harsh treatment.

³⁴ You will go mad because of all the tragedy you see around you.

³⁵ The LORD will cover your knees and legs with incurable boils. In fact, you will be covered from head to foot.

³⁶ "The LORD will exile you and your king to a nation unknown to you and your ancestors. There in exile you will worship gods of wood and stone!

³⁷ You will become an object of horror, ridicule, and mockery among all the nations to which the LORD sends you.

[38] "You will plant much but harvest little, for locusts will eat your crops.

[39] You will plant vineyards and care for them, but you will not drink the wine or eat the grapes, for worms will destroy the vines.

[40] You will grow olive trees throughout your land, but you will never use the olive oil, for the fruit will drop before it ripens.

[41] You will have sons and daughters, but you will lose them, for they will be led away into captivity.

[42] Swarms of insects will destroy your trees and crops.

[43] "The foreigners living among you will become stronger and stronger, while you become weaker and weaker.

[44] They will lend money to you, but you will not lend to them. They will be the head, and you will be the tail!

[45] "If you refuse to listen to the LORD your God and to obey the commands and decrees he has given you, all these curses will pursue and overtake you until you are destroyed.

[46] These horrors will serve as a sign and warning among you and your descendants forever.

[47] If you do not serve the LORD your God

with joy and enthusiasm for the abundant benefits you have received,

[48] you will serve your enemies whom the LORD will send against you. You will be left hungry, thirsty, naked, and lacking in everything. The LORD will put an iron yoke on your neck, oppressing you harshly until he has destroyed you.

[49] "The LORD will bring a distant nation against you from the end of the earth, and it will swoop down on you like a vulture. It is a nation whose language you do not understand,

[50] a fierce and heartless nation that shows no respect for the old and no pity for the young.

[51] Its armies will devour your livestock and crops, and you will be destroyed. They will leave you no grain, new wine, olive oil, calves, or lambs, and you will starve to death.

[52] They will attack your cities until all the fortified walls in your land—the walls you trusted to protect you—are knocked down. They will attack all the towns in the land the LORD your God has given you.

[53] "The siege and terrible distress of the enemy's attack will be so severe that you will eat the flesh of your own sons and

daughters, whom the LORD your God has given you.

⁵⁴ The most tenderhearted man among you will have no compassion for his own brother, his beloved wife, and his surviving children.

⁵⁵ He will refuse to share with them the flesh he is devouring—the flesh of one of his own children—because he has nothing else to eat during the siege and terrible distress that your enemy will inflict on all your towns.

⁵⁶ The most tender and delicate woman among you—so delicate she would not so much as touch the ground with her foot—will be selfish toward the husband she loves and toward her own son or daughter.

⁵⁷ She will hide from them the afterbirth and the new baby she has borne, so that she herself can secretly eat them. She will have nothing else to eat during the siege and terrible distress that your enemy will inflict on all your towns.

⁵⁸ "If you refuse to obey all the words of instruction that are written in this book, and if you do not fear the glorious and awesome name of the LORD your God,

⁵⁹ then the LORD will overwhelm you and your children with indescribable

plagues. These plagues will be intense and without relief, making you miserable and unbearably sick.

⁶⁰ He will afflict you with all the diseases of Egypt that you feared so much, and you will have no relief.

⁶¹ The LORD will afflict you with every sickness and plague there is, even those not mentioned in this Book of Instruction, until you are destroyed.

⁶² Though you become as numerous as the stars in the sky, few of you will be left because you would not listen to the LORD your God.

⁶³ "Just as the LORD has found great pleasure in causing you to prosper and multiply, the LORD will find pleasure in destroying you. You will be torn from the land you are about to enter and occupy.

⁶⁴ For the LORD will scatter you among all the nations from one end of the earth to the other. There you will worship foreign gods that neither you nor your ancestors have known, gods made of wood and stone!

⁶⁵ There among those nations you will find no peace or place to rest. And the LORD will cause your heart to tremble, your eyesight to fail, and your soul to despair.

⁶⁶ Your life will constantly hang in the

balance. You will live night and day in fear, unsure if you will survive.

[67] In the morning you will say, 'If only it were night!' And in the evening you will say, 'If only it were morning!' For you will be terrified by the awful horrors you see around you.

[68] Then the LORD will send you back to Egypt in ships, to a destination I promised you would never see again. There you will offer to sell yourselves to your enemies as slaves, but no one will buy you."
Deuteronomy 28:15–68 (NLT):

God Wants to Bless You, Not Curse You

Wow, what a horrifying list! You may look at this and ask, "How can a loving God do this to His own people?" God is holy and sin cannot stand in His presence. Sin is demonic—and harmful to all who are caught in its snare. God loved the children of Israel and wanted them to live in the good pleasures and blessings He wanted to give them. But, this could only happen if they obeyed His laws and instruction.

Suppose you have a 3-year-old son and you've told him over and over not to touch the hot stove. He disobeys and puts his little hand on that burner. Ouch! You didn't want him to get hurt, but because he didn't obey your instruction, he suffered the consequences of disobedience.

"Well, he's just a little boy," you might explain. "He

47

didn't understand the ramifications of his behavior." This is true, but the results are the same. Now, suppose you have a teenage daughter, who does understand right from wrong. You warn her not to hang out with a certain crowd. She sneaks out to a party where there's drinking going on. One of the boys, too drunk to drive, offers her a ride home, but on the way, a tragedy happens. He swerves on the road and hits another vehicle head on. They survive, but suffer severe, crippling injuries and long, painful months of recovery.

You love your daughter and you're heartbroken over the pain she's going through. If she had obeyed your warning, it never would have happened. God's laws—and even human laws—are made to keep people safe and ensure that they will enjoy a good life. So you see, God warns His people out of love and concern for their well-being, not because He is harsh or mean.

Key Points

- The curse of disobedience resulted from the fall of Adam.
- God's laws are given to protect His people and bless them.
- God instructs people in the best way for every situation.
- When a person obeys God, they will prosper in every area.
- God is love—He is not mean, but fair and just in all things.

Action Assignment:
If you have ever blamed God or others for bad things or

injustices that have happened to you, ask the Holy Spirit to change your mindset and shed God's love abroad in your heart (see Romans 5:5). Know that curses come from the devil, not God, and take responsibility for any part you've had in opening the door to allow the devil access to your thoughts, your words, or your actions. Say, "I love You Father, and I know that You love me no matter what. You proved it when You sent Jesus to die on the cross for my sins. Forgive me for doubting You and giving in to fear, bitterness, or any other negative emotion I've held in my heart against You or others."

Chapter 4

An Inventory of Blessings

In both Old and New Testaments we find important keys to receiving "The Blessing." God told Abram (Abraham) to leave his home and go to a country with which he wasn't familiar. Abraham didn't even know where he was going, but he trusted God, so he, his wife Sarah, and their nephew Lot, along with all their herdsmen, livestock and belongings, started out on this journey of faith.

> Now the Lord had said unto Abram, Get thee out of thy country, and from thy kindred, and from thy father's house, unto a land that I will shew thee: and I will make of thee a great nation, and I will bless thee, and make thy name great; and thou shalt be a blessing: and I will bless them that bless thee, and curse him that curseth thee: and in thee shall all families of the earth be blessed. (Genesis 12:1–3)

Receiving The Blessing
Key #1: Obedience

Because of Abraham's obedience, God promised to bless him and make him a great nation. What's more— all the families of the earth would be blessed because of faithful Abraham!

Though Abraham chose to be obedient to God's instructions, there are many who rebel against God. Do you remember the story of Saul, the king, in 1 Samuel, chapter 15? The Lord had instructed Saul to utterly destroy his enemies, the Amalekites, and all that they had, and not to take anything back from the battle. Did Saul obey? No. He spared the enemy king and took the best of the sheep, oxen, lambs and all that was good.

When Samuel confronted him, Saul said these animals were to sacrifice to the Lord. Sometimes we make excuses for not obeying God's Word that sound good to us, but God is not pleased. This is the message Samuel delivered to Saul:

> And Samuel said, Hath the LORD *as great* delight in burnt offerings and sacrifices, as in obeying the voice of the LORD? Behold, to obey *is* better than sacrifice, *and* to hearken than the fat of rams. For rebellion *is as* the sin of witchcraft, and stubbornness *is as* iniquity and idolatry. Because thou hast rejected the word of the LORD, he hath also rejected thee from *being* king. (1 Samuel 15:22–23)

Later in the life of Saul (see 1 Samuel, chapter 28), we see how he became fearful of losing a battle. The prophet Samuel had died, and Saul wanted advice from him, so he sought out a witch to "bring Samuel up from the dead." So you see, how diabolic the sin of rebellion is in that it leads even to witchcraft and opens the door to demonic activity.

Even today, we see rebellion toward God in high places such as government and other prominent areas of society. Those, who reject God and His Word, will lose their power and be destroyed at some point if they don't repent and turn to the Lord. The wicked may look like they're prospering or getting away with corruption, but they will be exposed and experience God's wrath. (To see what God says about the wicked, and how we should not allow them to cause us to sin but rather to wait upon God for His justice, see Psalm 37.)

Back to our story of how God called Abraham out of his "comfort zone" to travel to parts unknown. He was blessed to become a blessing to generations.

Key #2: Blessing Israel

Notice also that God promised to bless all who blessed Abraham, whose descendants later became the nation of Israel. So today, when we bless God's chosen people, the Jews, and their homeland, we will be blessed by God! (I might add here that this same principle applies in reverse. God said those who cursed Israel would themselves be cursed.)

Psalm 122:6 describes the benefit of blessing Israel,

"Pray for the peace of Jerusalem: they shall prosper that love thee." Do you want to prosper and be blessed? Pray, love and stand with the people of Israel!

"Aren't the blessings outlined in Deuteronomy 28 just for the people in Abraham's day...the people of the Old Testament?" you may ask. No! Speaking to the Galatian (New Testament) church, Paul said this about Abraham.

> [6] Even Abraham "believed God, and it was credited to him as righteousness."
> [7] Therefore know **that those who are of faith are the sons of Abraham.**
> [8] And the Scripture, foreseeing that God would justify the Gentiles by faith, preached the gospel in advance to Abraham, saying, **"In you shall all the nations be blessed."**
> [9] So then **those who are of faith are blessed with faithful Abraham.**
> [10] For all who rely on the works of the law are under the curse...(but)
> [13] Christ has redeemed us from the curse of the law by being made a curse for us—as it is written, "Cursed is everyone who hangs on a tree"—
> [14] so that **the blessing of Abraham might come on the Gentiles through Jesus Christ**, that we might receive the promise of the Spirit through faith.
> (Galatians 3:6–10, 13–14 MEV – emphasis mine)

If you are born again, you have been redeemed from the curse of the law and are eligible to receive the blessings of Abraham in Deuteronomy 28:

> [1] "If you fully obey the LORD your God and carefully keep all his commands that I am giving you today, the LORD your God will set you high above all the nations of the world.
>
> [2] You will experience all these blessings if you obey the LORD your God:
>
> [3] Your towns and your fields will be blessed.
>
> [4] Your children and your crops will be blessed.
>
> The offspring of your herds and flocks will be blessed.
>
> [5] Your fruit baskets and breadboards will be blessed.
>
> [6] Wherever you go and whatever you do, you will be blessed.
>
> [7] "The LORD will conquer your enemies when they attack you. They will attack you from one direction, but they will scatter from you in seven!
>
> [8] "The LORD will guarantee a blessing on everything you do and will fill your storehouses with grain. The LORD your God will bless you in the land he is giving you.
>
> [9] "If you obey the commands of the LORD

your God and walk in his ways, the LORD will establish you as his holy people as he swore he would do.

¹⁰ Then all the nations of the world will see that you are a people claimed by the LORD, and they will stand in awe of you.

¹¹ "The LORD will give you prosperity in the land he swore to your ancestors to give you, blessing you with many children, numerous livestock, and abundant crops.

¹² The LORD will send rain at the proper time from his rich treasury in the heavens and will bless all the work you do. You will lend to many nations, but you will never need to borrow from them.

¹³ If you listen to these commands of the LORD your God that I am giving you today, and if you carefully obey them, the LORD will make you the head and not the tail, and you will always be on top and never at the bottom.

¹⁴ You must not turn away from any of the commands I am giving you today, nor follow after other gods and worship them. (verses 1–14 NLT)

God Wants to Give You Favor and Blessing

How awesome are these blessings! Prosperity in your home, your family, your business, your bank accounts (storehouses), your food and all your property. You will have favor and blessing in all your dealings, everywhere you go and in everything you do. God will protect you from all your enemies and rescue you from attack. He will set you apart from those who don't know Him. He will make you the head and place you on top!

The blessings for obedience are amazing! Obedience is even a sign of our love for our Savior. Jesus said, "Those who truly love me are those who obey my commands. Whoever passionately loves me will be passionately loved by my Father. And I will passionately love you in return and will manifest my life within you" (John 14:21 TPT).

A Miracle Close to Home

Rev. Billy Ortiz relates a wonderful story in his book *Where Will the People You Meet Spend Eternity?* about his wife Josie's mom and entire family:

"I remember when Josie's mom was in bed and had not eaten for 17 days. The Holy Ghost said, 'Now is the time for her to give her heart to Jesus. Go pray for her and she'll eat.'

"You see, God will give you a word which is usually meant to give you, or somebody else, a breakthrough, and for a testimony of His goodness and power! Listen carefully for God's direction and you will be amazed at what He does!

"I jumped in the car and said to my wife, 'Come on, Honey. Let's go get your mom's favorite soup. We're going to go feed her.' The key is obedience. Josie said sadly, 'But she can't eat.'

"Full of trust and knowing I had heard from God and

having received that gift of grace and impartation of His faith, I spoke out confidently, 'She is going to eat tonight on her own!' We bought her favorite broccoli soup and my wife put it into the blender. When we got there, Mom was so weak and still in bed. I ran in there, in the Name of Jesus, and said, 'Hi, Mom.' I was praying in my prayer language and she just barely looked up at me. 'In the Name of Jesus, Mom,' I declared, 'Get up!' I stretched my hand out toward her, and immediately she sat straight up! She slung her feet over the side of the bed.

"Everybody started crying. They hadn't seen her move in 17 days. I said, 'Now, we're going to eat, Mom.' We put a towel on her lap, and my wife with tears in her eyes was filled with joy at seeing her mom start to eat again. She ate about three-quarters of that bowl of soup in only three minutes. Josie's mom lived for another six months—born again—before Jesus took her home to be with Him. Thank you, God.

"(But that's not the end of the story.) It's interesting that after this happened; her testimony was so powerful that the whole family, including Dad, got saved."

God Has a Miracle for Your Family, too

Don't give up. This will happen for your family, too. God will use you to stand in the gap for your family, and for many other precious people, too. He will use you to bring them into the kingdom. **You must simply obey the leading of the Spirit of God in you.**

Key Points

- The Church, like Israel, is a chosen people with a special destiny.
- You have been redeemed from the curse through Jesus Christ.
- If you are born again, you can receive the blessings of Abraham.
- God's blessings include healing, prosperity, provision and protection.
- Obedience is the key to receiving everything good from God.

Action Assignment:

Deuteronomy 30:19 gives a command to choose life or death, blessing or cursing. Say out loud, "Lord, I choose life and blessing!" Thank God for each blessing He has given you or placed in your life. Take time to play some worship music and soak in God's presence or sing a song of thanksgiving to your Father in heaven today. God inhabits our praises, and you will find the problems you face will become lighter or even disappear completely!

Chapter 5

Entering Your Promised Land

As a 6-year-old child, I spent much of my time in my room, writing stories and drawing pictures. I had a vivid imagination, and I found this more exciting than playing tag with the kids in the neighborhood. "When I grow up, I'm going to be a teacher," I thought to myself. "No, I think I'll be a writer."

I grew up...After quitting high school, my first job was in a suburban factory assembling parts, then in the mailroom followed by a promotion to be the receptionist in a downtown Chicago publishing company. I moved on from there to become a secretary, then a purchasing agent.

I had long since forgotten my childhood aspiration of being a teacher or a writer, and I reasoned, "I don't have enough education for those careers anyway." Sometime later, while I was looking for a new job, I volunteered in a Christian ministry I'd heard about that needed help in the office. I shared with my supervisor that I needed full-time work, so they connected me with their headquarters office in California, which just happened to have a position open.

A Dream Come True

Would you believe it—the job was for a writer AND editor position combined. I was interviewed, and despite my lack of both education and bona fide experience, I was hired on the spot for not just an entry-level position, but my new title would be Chief Editor and Writer. Wow, this was a blessing that I wasn't qualified for, but God had showered me with His favor and grace. He made my childhood dream come true and gave me the best salary I'd ever had prior to that job!

> "...For I know the plans I have for you,"
> declares the LORD, "plans to prosper you
> and not to harm you, plans to give you hope
> and a future" (Jeremiah 29:11 NIV).

It is not God's will that you live in debt, barely making it from one paycheck to the next. Or that your body is ravaged with cancer or some other debilitating disease. Or that your marriage falls apart and your children get into all kinds of trouble. Neither does He want your heart to be filled with fear and anxiety over your present circumstances or for you to be apprehensive about the future.

God's Plans for You Are Good

God's "plans (are) to give you hope and a future." This is the promise He made to Israel, while still in

Babylonian captivity, that their future was bright. Not only were His plans for them good, He was the One who would rescue them.

I declare over you today, **"God will rescue you out of every snare of the devil, every sickness and disease, every lack and bondage to debt, and every adverse situation you are facing."**

What will be your response when you see God's goodness in your life? "Then you will call on me and come and pray to me, and I will listen to you. You will seek me and find me when you seek me with all your heart" (Jeremiah 29:12–13). Just as you love it when your children show respect and affection toward you, our Father in heaven is thrilled when His children—you and me—"seek (Him) with all (our) heart."

God will not reject you like people sometimes do. He will not deride you, saying, "I didn't mean it" or "I was just kidding." No, you can depend on His promises. Get excited about what lies ahead for you. "Make God the utmost delight and pleasure of your life, and he will provide for you what you desire the most" (Psalm 37:4 TPT).

A Land of Giants

Do your problems sometimes seem like giants—too big to handle, too impossible to overcome? Well, the Israelites felt the same way. After releasing them from their captivity in Egypt and bringing them out to freedom, God promised to give them a new land...a land filled with "milk and honey" (all good things).

There was just one problem. There were still people living in the land where God was taking them. God told the leaders to go on a scouting expedition…to be of good courage and spy out the land to see if it was weak or strong, good or bad, and what its inhabitants were like. So, 12 men headed toward Canaan, the Promised Land, to check it out. As they explored, they discovered huge fruit growing in the land—pomegranates, figs and grapes, clusters so large it took two men to carry all of it back to the people.

The Report of the 10 Spies

Ten of the 12 spies were fearful of what they saw and came back with this negative report:

> "…We went into the land to which you sent us, and it does flow with milk and honey! Here is its fruit. But the people who live there are powerful, and the cities are fortified and very large. We even saw descendants of Anak there. The Amalekites live in the Negev; the Hittites, Jebusites and Amorites live in the hill country; and the Canaanites live near the sea and along the Jordan." (Numbers 13:27–29 NIV)

However, two of the 12 believed God, who had instructed the children of Israel to conquer the land and take possession of it for He had given it to them.

We Are Well Able to Overcome

Joshua and Caleb give a good report:

> Then Caleb silenced the people before Moses and said, "We should go up and take possession of the land, for we can certainly do it." But the men who had gone up with him said, "We can't attack those people; they are stronger than we are." And they spread among the Israelites a bad report about the land they had explored. They said, "The land we explored devours those living in it. All the people we saw there are of great size. We saw the Nephilim there (the descendants of Anak come from the Nephilim). We seemed like grasshoppers in our own eyes, and we looked the same to them." (verses 30–33)

Have you ever felt as little as a "grasshopper" in the sight of your problem or challenge? You're not alone. I have. I think most everyone has at one time or another. While the 12 leaders of Israel were all impressed with the good provisions and blessings of the land, only two leaders, Joshua and Caleb, put their trust in God. They believed that though they were limited in their own natural strength and size, through God's power the victory would be won.

Don't Let Earthly Limitations Stop You

Do you see yourself as unable to enter the "promised land" God has for you? Maybe you feel you're not strong enough, not educated enough, not attractive enough, or that you don't have the money, a "good enough" credit score, or the connections needed to complete what God is telling you to do.

My friend, you are a child of God! You are living in the world, but you're not limited by the world. At the beginning of His earthly ministry, "Jesus began to preach, and to say, Repent: for the kingdom of heaven is at hand" (Matthew 4:17). We sometimes think that "repent" just means to feel sorry about something we did or said, but it's much more than that. It denotes a change of mind, a desire and willingness to turn around and go in a new direction.

A Change of Mind

Yes, we need to repent to God, and to those we've hurt, for the bad things we said or did, but there's more. Often, we need to repent about what we didn't say or didn't do. Did you ever fail to take advantage of an opportunity to share the good news about Jesus with someone, pray for a coworker, or help a neighbor? I have, and I regretted it deeply.

Beyond this, how about repenting for not trusting God like the 10 spies failed to do? How about repenting when we've said, " I can't. I'm not (fill in the blank) enough," or "I don't have the education, money (or whatever) to do this."? Doubting God is just as much sin as telling a lie. Because basically, you are telling a lie on God, even if it's only to yourself. You're saying that God isn't big enough to bring to pass what He's promised.

Say this with me now, "Father, I repent for not believing You about (name the source of your doubt). I know with You nothing is impossible. Right now, I purpose in my heart to put my trust in You to bring (name it) to pass in my life. In Jesus' Name, Amen."

You Are a Citizen of God's Kingdom

It's important enough to repeat: "You are living in the world, but you're not limited by the world." Why did Jesus tell people to repent? "Because "the kingdom of heaven is at hand." Know this, you are a citizen of God's kingdom, the kingdom of heaven.

Think about this for a moment. Is there sickness in heaven...sorrow in heaven...pain in heaven...lack or want in heaven...anger or strife in heaven...anxiety, depression or fear in heaven? A resounding NO! The disciples asked Jesus to teach them how to pray.

> He said to them, "When you pray, say: Our Father, who is in heaven, hallowed be Your name. Your kingdom come; **Your will be done on earth, as it is in heaven.** Give us each day our daily bread. And forgive us our sins, for we also forgive everyone who is indebted to us. And lead us not into temptation, but deliver us from evil." (Luke 11:2–4 MEV)

The scripture says, "Your will be done on earth, as it

is in heaven." This is the kingdom of God. Notice some of the things of heaven that are supposed to now be on earth: provision (our daily bread), forgiveness (our own and others), and protection (from temptation and evil). This would include everything evil, not just danger, but sickness, sorrow, shame, lack, poverty, anger, strife, broken relationships, everything that is not good.

Everything Good Comes from Heaven

James 1:17 in *The Passion Translation* declares that "Every gift God freely gives us is good and perfect, streaming down from the Father of lights, who shines from the heavens with no hidden shadow or darkness and is never subject to change." Everything good in your life and mine comes from God's kingdom, the kingdom of heaven. This is a forever promise—God never changes!

God is calling you to enter into your promised land, just like He had planned for the Israelites to do. But, we have an advantage over those in the Old Covenant. Jesus came to earth so that through His sacrifice we could be made the righteousness of God in Him through the forgiveness of sin. Jesus made it possible for us to become citizens in the kingdom of God and enjoy all the good plans and purposes God has destined for us—here on the earth and for all eternity.

The Kingdom of Heaven Has Its Privileges

God has called you to a life of peace, joy, good health, prosperity, provision of all your needs, protection, all of your family saved and walking in God's good promises, and having more than enough to give to the work of God, enjoy His blessings, and help others.

You have been empowered with wisdom, revelation knowledge and understanding. You can see things worldly people, who do not know God, cannot see. Because with this supernatural knowledge, you can solve problems others don't understand. As a kingdom citizen, you receive favor. Contrary to human reasoning, you walk according to God's Word, and you will have good success. (See Joshua 1:8.)

Key Points

- The plans and purposes of God for your life are good.
- Whatever "giants" you face, you can defeat them in the Lord.
- You are a citizen of God's kingdom with all of its privileges.
- God has called you to a life of peace, joy and blessing.
- It's time to enter into your "promised land."

Action Assignment:

No matter what the circumstances look like or how you feel, remember that God has good plans for your life (see Jeremiah 29:11), and He wants to bless you. Take some time to write down in your journal the good plans and promises God has spoken to your heart or that you find in His Word. Say, "Dear God, I'm sorry if I doubted you or let fear rob me of my joy. I believe Your plans for me are good. Renew my faith and hope in Your promises."

Chapter 6

The Secret Place of Success

While we have received salvation through the cross of Christ, God's promises are not automatic. Have you ever experienced victory in one area of your life and something else seems to fall apart?

Praise God, I got healed…I got a new house…I got that promotion at work! That's wonderful! But then, another ailment appears in your body, your children are acting up, or you discover termites in your new home. So, you say, "Now what else can happen to me?" Or, "Not again—things were going so great. How could this problem come back?"

That's a good question…I thought I was healed by the stripes of Jesus. I thought God was protecting my family, finances and property. I thought all I had to do was have faith. Yes, but…in his book, James clarifies this issue about faith.

> What does it profit, my brethren, if someone
> says he has faith but does not have works?
> Can faith save him? If a brother or sister is
> naked and destitute of daily food, and one
> of you says to them, "Depart in peace, be
> warmed and filled," but you do not give
> them the things which are needed for the
> body, what does it profit? Thus also faith
> by itself, if it does not have works, is dead.
> (James 2:14–17 NKJV)

Are You a Friend of God?

The key is not that we have faith, but Who we have faith in. Faith requires relationship. Further in James, chapter 2, it says "'Abraham believed God, and it was accounted to him for righteousness.' And he was called the friend of God" (verse 23). Relationship is personal and intimate, not just religious duty. God wants our worship and obedience; yes, but more than that, He longs for relationship. He wants us to come to Him daily, not just on Sundays, to spend time with Him as you would with your best friend.

Our lives are busy and our schedules overflowing with commitments difficult to keep up with. But, if we want to receive God's best for our lives and fulfill His glorious destiny for us, then we had better pencil in quality time to get to know Him and hear His voice. This is the only way we can know His will and receive the valuable instruction and impartation from the Holy Spirit that we need to walk daily in His blessings.

Psalm 91, often called the protection psalm, gives us an

enlightening description of what we can expect from God when we meet Him in the "secret place." I try to pray this, along with other scriptures, every day, because I believe God's Word has the power to keep us secure from all harm and manifest every blessing He has provided as we draw close to Him. Make this scripture personal to you and your family. And, make it your daily confession, too:

The Secret Place

¹ He who dwells in the secret place of the Most High shall remain stable and fixed under the shadow of the Almighty [Whose power no foe can withstand].

² I will say of the Lord, He is my Refuge and my Fortress, my God; on Him I lean and rely, and in Him I [confidently] trust!

³ For [then] He will deliver you from the snare of the fowler and from the deadly pestilence.

⁴ [Then] He will cover you with His pinions, and under His wings shall you trust and find refuge; His truth and His faithfulness are a shield and a buckler.

⁵ You shall not be afraid of the terror of the night, nor of the arrow (the evil plots and slanders of the wicked) that flies by day,

⁶ Nor of the pestilence that stalks in darkness, nor of the destruction and sudden death that surprise and lay waste at noonday.

⁷ A thousand may fall at your side, and ten

thousand at your right hand, but it shall not come near you.

8 Only a spectator shall you be [yourself inaccessible in the secret place of the Most High] as you witness the reward of the wicked.

9 Because you have made the Lord your refuge, and the Most High your dwelling place,

10 There shall no evil befall you, nor any plague or calamity come near your tent.

11 For He will give His angels [especial] charge over you to accompany and defend and preserve you in all your ways [of obedience and service].

12 They shall bear you up on their hands, lest you dash your foot against a stone.

13 You shall tread upon the lion and adder; the young lion and the serpent shall you trample underfoot.

14 Because he has set his love upon Me, therefore will I deliver him; I will set him on high, because he knows and understands My name [has a personal knowledge of My mercy, love, and kindness—trusts and relies on Me, knowing I will never forsake him, no, never].

15 He shall call upon Me, and I will answer him; I will be with him in trouble, I will deliver him and honor him.

¹⁶ With long life will I satisfy him and show
him My salvation.
(Psalm 91:1–16 AMPC)

Notice the word "pestilence." This refers to plagues
and pandemics such as the coronavirus.

Supernatural Protection and Provision

I won't recap all the blessings and benefits we receive
in this psalm because we've already listed many in the
last chapter. However, let's look more closely at a couple
verses. In today's world, there are many dangers, terror
and tragedies that occur, sometimes very close to home.
Verses 5–7 promise safety in the midst of a terror threat,
a hurricane, or a mass shooting. Though others all around
you, great masses of people, come to harm, you will go
through it untouched. Why? Because you've made the Lord
your dwelling place, and the enemy can't touch you there.

Angelic Intervention

Verse 11 assures us that our angels stand guard over
our lives, ready to defend and protect us. (See chapter 9,
"New Age, Demons and Angelic Intervention" for more
on angels and the spiritual realm.)

I remember a time of supernatural protection. I was
visiting homes in the neighborhood in behalf of a local
church. Walking up a long, steep set of stairs with no railing
or anything to hold on to, I got to the top of the stairway
and knocked on the door. A man answered, "Yes, can I help
you?" I was about to explain the reason I was there, when

all of a sudden, a little boy, probably no more than four, raced forcefully toward the open doorway. It startled me, and I started to lose my balance and fall backward, when I felt a presence holding me in place. I didn't see anyone, but I'm convinced it was an angel that arrived on the scene just at the perfect time to protect not only me, but the little boy who showed no signs of stopping short of the doorway.

Another time, a lady ran a stop light and plowed into my car at 50 mph or so. The car was totaled and towed away, but I walked out of it with minimal injuries. One of the policemen at the scene told me, "You are very lucky. Most people die in crashes this bad." But, I knew better... It was another angelic intervention!

You Have Power Over the Enemy

Now, look at verse 13...lions and snakes are scary, and in the natural, we don't have much defense against them, but in the "secret place" where we have communed with God and received His anointing, we have the power to overcome even lions and snakes. I believe here also, the "serpent" can refer to Satan, our adversary. In the secret place, we are fortified with spiritual might and wisdom as we soak in the presence of the Lord, and the devil is no match for us. Luke 10:19 confirms this, "Behold, I (Jesus) give unto you power to tread on serpents and scorpions, and over all the power of the enemy: and nothing shall by any means hurt you."

God Promises a Long and Satisfying Life

Finally in verse 16, what an awesome promise—He

will satisfy us with long life and show us His salvation (in Greek, "sozo," which means to save, deliver, protect, heal, preserve, and to make whole).

Wow! What a phenomenal promise of divine protection. Some things that could potentially harm us, God never allows to get near us or cross our path. At other times, He will deliver us out of the danger or from attack. If you follow the conditions of this psalm, God promises to keep you, your family, your house and your possessions safe, free from sickness and loss. Sound too good to be true? It's not! Change your thinking—ALL things are possible with God!

Dwelling in the Secret Place with God

Keep in mind, this promise is for believers who walk daily in their covenant relationship with Jesus, whose minds and hearts are fixed upon Him, who obey the voice of the Holy Spirit within them when He tells them, "Do this," or "Don't do that...don't go there," and so forth. God speaks to us in a still, small voice. When we listen and obey, we are protected and can receive whatever we need.

God promises help to those who seek Him in the "secret place." Communicate with God daily in prayer as you would talk with your best friend. Spend time thanking and praising God; cultivate an awareness of God's presence as you go about your day's activities. Study, believe, and act on what you see in the Word of God.

You will discover a new peace, joy, spiritual understanding and boldness as you spend time with God in the "secret place." You will begin to experience greater fulfillment and success in your family, finances, job and ministry. In the secret place of God's presence is His glory and His power. How can any curse stand in the presence of God? It can't! It must flee from you and set you free!

Key Points
- Spending time with God in the "secret place" brings great reward.
- As you commune with the Lord, He promises never to forsake you.
- His presence brings fullness of joy, peace and strength to you.
- God gives you power to overcome every enemy.
- You will receive greater spiritual understanding and boldness.

Action Assignment:
Speak out loud Psalm 91 today and every day, substituting your name, "I" and "me" wherever applicable to make the wonderful promises in this psalm personal to you, your family and your situation. If you've been feeling fearful, stressed, depressed or overburdened, remember that a merry heart is good medicine. Stop rehearsing your problems and just laugh! Even if it's hard or seems fake, just keep laughing. It will soon become real and take the heavy load off of you. Cast your care on Jesus and rest in Him. (See 1 Peter 5:7 and Matthew 11:29–30.)

Chapter 7

God Is Doing a New Thing in Your Life

Are you ready for something new? Has God given you a vision and purpose for your life that you haven't yet seen come to pass? Do the problems of life weigh you down and wear you out, so you have no drive or desire to pursue God's promises?

> Therefore, since we are surrounded by so great a cloud of witnesses [who by faith have testified to the truth of God's absolute faithfulness], **stripping off every unnecessary weight** and the sin which so easily and cleverly entangles us, **let us run with endurance and active persistence** the race that is set before us, (Hebrews 12:1 AMP – emphasis mine)

A runner must be sure that he is carrying no extra

weight on himself that could slow him down. So, too, we must be free of anything that would prevent or hinder us from fulfilling God's plans and purposes. In addition, a runner must not quit or give up if he (or she) wants to win the prize for which they are competing. You and I must also run our race with endurance and persistence, overcoming every adversity and obstacle that arises.

How do we run—and win—this "God-ordained race" that He has set before each of us? Faith! Hebrews 12:1, which we just read, follows chapter 11, widely known as the "Faith Hall of Fame." The list includes many heroes of faith from both the Old and New Testaments, who ran their races faithfully, enduring much hardship, believing God even when they didn't understand why or couldn't see ahead into the future…to the day of Messiah's coming to earth.

Hebrews 12 continues (verse 2)…

> [**looking away from all that will distract us** and] **focusing our eyes on Jesus**, who is **the Author and Perfecter of faith** [the first incentive for our belief and the One who brings our faith to maturity], who for the joy [of accomplishing the goal] set before Him endured the cross, disregarding the shame, and sat down at the right hand of the throne of God [revealing His deity, His authority, and the **completion of His work**]. (AMP – emphasis mine)

It is vitally important that we do not allow anything or anyone to distract us from running this "faith race" by keeping our eyes on Jesus, not on the earthly pursuits, trials and temptations. We can't be looking to the left or the right, or glancing behind us to compare ourselves with others, but our focus must be straight ahead, just like a runner, to the accomplishment of the goals God has given us.

Running the Race for an Eternal Gold Crown

In order to complete His work on the earth, Jesus endured shame and unimaginable pain. But despite these earthly obstacles and hardships, Jesus won the victory (for us). Now, He sits at the right hand of His Father, still interceding for you and me, rooting us on in our race, and enabling us to persevere and reach the goal line. We must run the race God has set before us like a disciplined athlete "who does it to get a crown that will not last, but we do it to get a crown that will last forever" (1 Corinthians 9:25 NIV).

We Are Living in a Prophetic Season

It's imperative that we stay alert and aware of what's going on in the world. Not only with our natural mind, but we need supernatural eyesight. This is no time to be asleep spiritually.

[1] But as to the suitable times and the precise seasons and dates, brethren, you have no necessity for anything being written to you. [2] For you yourselves know perfectly well that the day of the [return of the] Lord will

come [as unexpectedly and suddenly] as a thief in the night.

³ When people are saying, All is well and secure, and, There is peace and safety, then in a moment unforeseen destruction (ruin and death) will come upon them as suddenly as labor pains come upon a woman with child; and they shall by no means escape, for there will be no escape.

⁴ But you are not in [given up to the power of] darkness, brethren, for that day to overtake you by surprise like a thief.

⁵ For you are all sons of light and sons of the day; we do not belong either to the night or to darkness.

⁶ Accordingly then, let us not sleep, as the rest do, but let us keep wide awake (alert, watchful, cautious, and on our guard) and let us be sober (calm, collected, and circumspect). (1 Thessalonians 5:1–6 AMPC)

Is Jesus Really Coming Back?

"Is Jesus really coming back?" you may wonder. Some scoff, "People have been saying that for centuries, and He hasn't come back yet!" The Bible is not a book of opinion—it's a book of truth. Not one of its thousands of prophecies will fail.

Consider the following, staggering, statistics compiled by noted Bible prophecy experts, Dr. Jack Van Impe and his wife Rexella, who have a Bible prophecy television program and worldwide internet media broadcasts on which they teach that Jesus is coming soon!

Dr. Van Impe comments in his *Prophecy 21st Century Revelations* video that there are 10,385 verses on Bible prophecy—the things to come—out of a total 165,000 scripture verses in the Bible itself. This means that one out of every 16 Bible verses is prophetic. Dr. Van Impe further states that there are 300 prophecies on the first coming of Christ, with a 20 to 1 ratio of prophecies concerning the second coming of Christ. **That's 6,000 prophecies that tell us Jesus is coming again—and He's coming soon!**

What's more, these end-time prophecies are found not only in the book of Revelation, but they abound in the Old Testament and New Testament as well.

God Is Doing a New Thing

Isaiah prophesies to the children of Israel that God is going to do a new thing in their nation and in their lives. "Do not remember the former things, Or ponder the things of the past. Listen carefully, I am about to do a new thing, Now it will spring forth; Will you not be aware of it? I will even put a road in the wilderness, Rivers in the desert" (Isaiah 43:18–19 AMP).

Paul, too, shares the importance of seeking the new thing God is doing in our lives, "Brothers, I do not count myself to have attained, but this one thing I do, forgetting those things which are behind and reaching forward to those things which are ahead, I press toward the goal to the prize of the high calling of God in Christ Jesus" (Philippians 3:13–14 MEV).

No Longer "Business as Usual"

We're living in a season, where it isn't "business as usual" anymore, and everything we plan or do must be viewed through the lens of the appearance of our soon-coming King, Jesus Christ. (Read more about this later.)

In order for God to do the "new thing" He has planned for you and me, we must be watchful. We must pray like we've never prayed before and live with an attitude of expectancy for our God to move and answer the prayers of His people, who are crying out to Him for this generation.

The Bible says, "It is impossible to please God without faith." Faith is vitally important if we are to receive healing, deliverance, family restoration, financial breakthroughs, business and career success, and overcome the curses, plagues and pandemonium we see all around us. Jesus said again and again, "Be it to you according to your faith."

It's Harvest Time

As critical as faith is to our receiving what we're believing for, I believe the Lord has been showing me how essential our focus is. With Jesus coming soon and the chaotic state our world is in, the focus of our attention and efforts has to enlarge. We can no longer be self-centered.

Matthew 9:36–38 in the *Modern English Version* says, "But when He (Jesus) saw the crowds, He was moved with compassion for them, because they fainted and were scattered, like sheep without a shepherd. Then He said to His disciples, 'The harvest truly is plentiful, but the laborers are few. Therefore, pray to the Lord of the harvest, that He will send out laborers into His harvest.'"

You've heard it said, "God will do for you what you do for others." When we show compassion and caring for our own family, our brothers and sisters in Christ, and those in the world that are hurting, spiritually blind and lost, God will meet our needs and answer our prayers. So, one key to overcoming whatever sickness, loss, lack or trial you're going through is to forget about your need and focus on helping others.

In the Psalms, it says that a person who "wins souls is wise." There is a soul winner's crown awaiting that person in heaven. God responds to you and me when our heart and hands are devoted to working in His harvest field.

A New Outlook

Faith cannot be simply intellectual assent. Faith has to be real, alive and birthed out of our heart. The Bible shows us how, "So then faith cometh by hearing, and hearing by the word of God" (Romans 10:17). The Word of God has to fill our heart to produce the faith that brings results. Then, that faith in our heart has to come forth in our conversation, "...for out of the abundance of our heart the mouth speaketh" (Matthew 12:34).

This is a profound, but oft-repeated, principle that will work if we work it! God's Word in our heart...faith is developed...it comes out our mouth...we receive that for which we have believed. It isn't complicated. This is the way God's kingdom works. (See Mark 11:22–25.)

You and I are passing through this earth, but we are not bound by man's limitations, worldly perspectives, or the (evil) powers and principalities of the demonic spirit realm.

We are citizens of the kingdom of heaven, and with God all things are possible! This is the new mindset we must put on...the new outlook we must embrace if we are to survive and be effective for the kingdom of God in this day.

"I Leave You My Peace"

The last thing I want to talk about in this chapter is how absolutely necessary the peace of God is to walking in faith and victory. In John, chapter 14, Jesus is speaking to His disciples, "But the Comforter, which is the Holy Ghost, whom the Father will send in my name, he shall teach you all things, and bring all things to your remembrance, whatsoever I have said unto you. Peace I leave with you, my peace I give unto you: not as the world giveth, give I unto you. Let not your heart be troubled, neither let it be afraid" (verses 26–27).

In this scene, Jesus is soon to go to be with His Father. He is letting His disciples, who depended so much on Him, know that He will send them another One in His place. Who would it be? The Holy Spirit! He will comfort them and teach them all things they need to know to walk according to God's will. The same Holy Spirit is at work in the lives of believers today.

Jesus is saying in essence, "Let go of your cares. Rest in Me; My peace will keep your heart from being troubled."

Let Peace Be Your Guide

Peace isn't just a "feel-good" feeling; it's a powerful fruit of the Spirit that will guide you when you have a decision to make. Peace will remove confusion, keep you on the right path, and prevent you from making mistakes. Peace will relieve the stress that so often causes sickness and anxiety, and drives us to speak foolish words and take desperate actions.

There's a difference between the peace of Jesus and the world's kind of peace that is built on man-centered values stemming from a sin-cursed, worldly belief system. Listen to the viewpoints of much of the media and mainstream secular society today…Right is wrong and wrong is right. Good is evil and evil is good. Those who don't know or refuse to believe God's value system (the Bible) think they are being moral, but it is a morality system that comes straight from hell. "Once you were under God's curse, doomed forever for your sins. You went along with the crowd and were just like all the others, full of sin, obeying Satan, the mighty prince of the power of the air, who is at work right now in the hearts of those who are against the Lord" (Ephesians 2:1–2 TLB).

How different is the peace that comes from our Lord: "Let the peace of Christ [the inner calm of one who walks daily with Him] be the controlling factor in your hearts [deciding and settling questions that arise]. To this peace indeed you were called as members in one body [of believers]. And be thankful [to God always]" (Colossians 3:15 AMP).

Peace takes away fear, "He shall not be afraid of evil tidings: his heart is fixed, trusting in the Lord. His heart is established, he shall not be afraid…" (Psalm 112:7–8 MEV). The Hebrew word meaning peace is "shalom," which means far more than just the absence of fear or anxiety. Shalom encompasses peace, health, prosperity, undisturbed well-being and wholeness—nothing missing and nothing broken.

Jesus is called the "Prince of Peace." When you spend time with Jesus, you cannot help but draw His peace into yourself, and as you yield to the Holy Spirit, the peace of Jesus will flow outward toward others.

Key Points
- God wants to do something new in your life.
- We need a new outlook and real faith for victory.
- We must enlarge our focus—It's harvest time!
- Jesus has sent the Holy Spirit to tell you all things.
- Jesus' peace is perfect, not as the peace the world gives.

Action Assignment:
Ask the Lord to give you a new vision, a new dream (whether awake or asleep), for what He has for you in this season. Get quiet before God, spend time listening for His voice; then meditate on whatever scriptures the Holy Spirit brings to your remembrance and follow the instructions He gives to you. Like Mary told the servants at the wedding described in John 2:5, "Whatever He says to you, do *it*."

Chapter 8

The Battle Is On, but You Win

Whether you are believing for victory in a battle for your mind, your health, your family, your finances or any other area, your warfare strategy is found in the Word of God. We have an enemy, who is trying to steal the blessings of God from us, but it's not your spouse or boss or next-door neighbor…it's not even the IRS or a scammer on the internet.

> For though we live in the world, we do not wage war as the world does. **The weapons we fight with are not the weapons of the world.** On the contrary, they have divine power to demolish strongholds. We demolish arguments and every pretension that sets itself up against the knowledge of God, and **we take captive every thought to make it obedient to Christ.** (2 Corinthians 10:3–5 NIV – emphasis mine)

Notice, our weapons are not of the world, instead they are spiritual. God is on your side and He will fight your battles. No one can stand against you because God is with you and for you. (See 2 Chronicles 20 and Romans 8:31.)

As mentioned in the previous chapter, it is vital that we have a new mindset, a right mindset, one that agrees with the Word of God. You've, no doubt, heard it said, "The mind is the battlefield (or playground) of the enemy, who is Satan, our adversary." Our thought life has everything to do with whether we achieve victory against the devil. That's why we must "take captive every thought to make it obedient to Christ." Jesus Christ is the living Word of God, "In the beginning [before all time] was the Word (Christ), and the Word was with God, and the Word was God Himself" (John 1:1 AMPC).

How to Stand Against the Enemy
Who Is Trying to Steal Your Healing, Family,
Finances, Business, Job or Ministry

In the game of football or any other team sport, which is the most important—the offense or the defense? The answer is both! If you have a history-making quarterback and offense racking up dozens of points, that's great, but you may still lose if the other team (your adversary) scores even more points because your defense is weak and can't stop them. On the other hand, if you have a fierce defense, you may keep the other team's score down, but if your own offense is lacking, you won't score enough points to win.

Just like in a football game, you as a believer have an

adversary, the devil, who is trying to block your victory. In this book, we are learning how to "defend" our territory—how to stand against everything the devil throws at us. Be encouraged! You and I don't have to cover all the defensive positions in our own strength or ability. The armor of God has us covered (more about this in the next chapter)!

The Best Defense Is a Good Offense

Jesus is your Quarterback, and you can be sure He won't succumb to defeat. He never loses anything! The Gospel of Luke describes the game plan (mission) of Jesus:

> "The Spirit of the LORD is upon Me, Because He has anointed Me To preach the gospel to the poor; He has sent Me to heal the brokenhearted, To proclaim liberty to the captives And recovery of sight to the blind, To set at liberty those who are oppressed; To proclaim the acceptable year of the LORD." (Luke 4:18–19, NKJV)

This scripture is the mission of Jesus upon the earth. We know His Word is true, so when the symptoms or circumstances say differently, we know that they are a lie.

The Devil is a Liar

John 8:44 speaks plainly, "For you are the children of your father the devil, and you love to do the evil things he does. He was a murderer from the beginning. He has always hated the truth, because there is no truth in him.

When he lies, it is consistent with his character; for he is a liar and the father of lies" (NLT).

What does this scripture tell us about the devil? He is a liar and cannot tell anything except lies. The devil hates the truth (the Word, both written and living; Jesus is the Truth) and those who stand in the truth (believers). And even worse, the devil is a murderer!

The devil is your enemy. He is the perpetrator behind everything evil, everything stolen, and everything contrary to the promises of God for your life. He is the one that makes you sick, causes strife in your family or on the job, steals your finances and executes "Murphy's law" in your daily circumstances. "The thief comes only in order to steal and kill and destroy. I (Jesus) came that they may have and enjoy life, and have it in abundance (to the full, till it overflows)" (John 10:10 AMPC).

Satan's Modus Operandi

Whatever you have received from God, whatever answer to prayer you need, or whatever unmet need you are believing for God to fulfill…Satan will try to interfere, to keep you from receiving; then, when you have received the promised blessing, he will try to take it from you or make you lose it!

The devil is the father of lies. He will put negative thoughts in your mind, "You're not really healed. Nothing happened when they prayed," or "You're going to wind up out on the streets. God's not going to help you," or "You're not good enough; You don't deserve it," or "He did it for others, but not for you."

Secondly, he will try to steal it from you, either by lying to you, getting others to come against you, or causing you to suffer loss, lack, sickness, broken relationships or other adverse circumstances.

Thirdly, both of the scriptures we read call the devil a murderer. He will try to kill or destroy your relationship with God and others, your mind, emotions or body, your finances, job, your home or other things you hold dear.

How Do We Overcome the Enemy?

Be alert, watchful and strong in faith. Don't get distracted or weighed down by your problems. Keep your eyes fixed on Jesus and stand firm in your faith. "Give all your worries and cares to God, for he cares about you. Stay alert! Watch out for your great enemy, the devil. He prowls around like a roaring lion, looking for someone to devour. Stand firm against him, and be strong in your faith…" (1 Peter 5:7–9, NLT).

Repent. We all miss it or mess up sometimes, no matter how hard we try to do right. God is merciful and kind. He gives us chance after chance after chance. Throughout the Gospels after healing various people, Jesus said, "Go and sin no more." Why? Because sin separates people from God, "But your iniquities have separated you from your God; And your sins have hidden His face from you, So that He will not hear" (Isaiah 59:2, NKJV).

It is not your own willpower that will deliver you from sin; it's the power of the Holy Spirit that you can depend on to set you free. Sin brings unwanted consequences, "For the wages of sin is death, but the

93

gift of God is eternal life in Christ Jesus our Lord" (Romans 6:23, NKJV).

When we repent, God gives us a fresh start. "If we confess our sins, He is faithful and just to forgive us our sins and to cleanse us from all unrighteousness" (1 John 1:9, NKJV).

How Did Jesus Overcome?

Even Jesus had to overcome the devil before He began His earthly ministry. Jesus was tempted by Satan, who promised to give Him the kingdoms of this world, if He would bow down and worship him. This would eliminate the suffering that lay ahead and bypass the work of the cross, but Jesus refused. He loved you and me too much to leave us in our sin.

Being baptized by John, Jesus identified with man. He was no longer *only* the Son of God, but now He had at the same time become the Son of man. It was time for Jesus' ministry upon the earth to begin, but first He had a test to pass.

> [1] Then Jesus, being filled with the Holy Spirit, returned from the Jordan and was led by the Spirit into the wilderness,
> [2] being tempted for forty days by the devil. And in those days He ate nothing, and afterward, when they had ended, He was hungry.
> [3] And the devil said to Him, "If You are the Son of God, command this stone to become bread."

⁴ But Jesus answered him, saying, "It is written, 'Man shall not live by bread alone, but by every word of God.'"

⁵ Then the devil, taking Him up on a high mountain, showed Him all the kingdoms of the world in a moment of time.

⁶ And the devil said to Him, "All this authority I will give You, and their glory; for this has been delivered to me, and I give it to whomever I wish.

⁷ Therefore, if You will worship before me, all will be Yours."

⁸ And Jesus answered and said to him, "Get behind Me, Satan! For it is written, 'You shall worship the LORD your God, and Him only you shall serve.'"

⁹ Then he brought Him to Jerusalem, set Him on the pinnacle of the temple, and said to Him, "If You are the Son of God, throw Yourself down from here.

¹⁰ For it is written: ' He shall give His angels charge over you, To keep you,'

¹¹ and, ' In their hands they shall bear you up, Lest you dash your foot against a stone.'"

¹² And Jesus answered and said to him, "It has been said, 'You shall not tempt the LORD your God.'"

¹³ Now when the devil had ended every temptation, he departed from Him until an opportune time." (Luke 4:1–13 NKJV)

How to Gain Victory Over Satan

The devil, whom we've already established as a liar, tried to get Jesus to abort God's plan for Him to save mankind. Notice that this portion of scripture gives several key principles for victory over the evil Satan: Live by the Word of God (verse 4), walk in faith and obedience (verse 4), command the devil to leave (verse 8), worship God (verse 8) and refuse to tempt or test God (verse 12).

Throughout these verses, you'll see a common thread. Jesus continually referred to the Word of God, saying, "It is written." When we are standing against the enemy who is trying to steal our healing or victory from us, we must stand firm in two things: First, stand firm in our confession. Listen to what our tongues are saying. Do our words line up with what the Word of God says?

Have you ever sat in a doctor's office and filled out a form that included writing down what diseases were prevalent in your family line? Have you then said, "My dad died from cancer. I suppose I'll get it too."? Repent from saying those words! If you're born again, you have a new DNA...you have a new Father. Through the blood of Christ, you are free from genetic diseases and generational curses. You have God's promise in Isaiah 53:4–5.

> Surely He has borne our griefs (sicknesses, weaknesses, and distresses) and carried our sorrows and pains [of punishment], yet we [ignorantly] considered Him stricken, smitten, and afflicted by God [as if with

leprosy]. But He was wounded for our transgressions, He was bruised for our guilt and iniquities; the chastisement [needful to obtain] peace and well-being for us was upon Him, and **with the stripes [that wounded] Him we are healed and made whole.** (AMPC – emphasis mine)

This last sentence is confirmed again in 1 Peter 2:24, "who Himself bore our sins in His own body on the tree, that we, having died to sins, might live for righteousness— **by whose stripes you were healed**" (NKJV – emphasis mine). Notice, here it says "were healed" so we know that it's not that you're going to be healed, but the healing already took place—at the cross! You just have to receive it NOW by faith. If you don't yet see the healing manifested in your body, don't give up. Don't think, "I guess I didn't get healed." Keep speaking God's Word. It *will* happen because "God is not a man, so he does not lie. He is not human, so he does not change his mind. Has he ever spoken and failed to act? Has he ever promised and not carried it through?" (Numbers 23:19 NLT).

Stop Those Negative Words

If our words are not lining up with God's Word, we need to get the negative words (and thoughts) OUT and make room for God's Word ONLY in our mind, heart and mouth.

And secondly, we must stand firm in "living" the Word of God through obedience and faith to "every word of

God." Check our schedules. Have we become too busy? Have other things crowded out our time in God's Word, studying, praying and confessing His good promises?

Choose to Speak Words of Faith

Faith speaks! Faith is not mental assent or willpower; rather, faith speaks TRUTH, what God's Word says, not what we fear or how things appear or what even our trusted friends advise. Jesus was never moved by outward circumstances, but He spoke only what He heard His Father say. Go with me to Matthew, chapter 9.

This is the story of the 12-year-old girl who became sick and died. Her father went to get Jesus and pleaded with Him to pray for her. When Jesus arrived at the house, mourners were all around, crying and carrying on. He put everybody, who was saying she was dead, out of the house and, "He said to them, 'Depart. **The girl is not dead, but is sleeping**...' And they laughed Him to scorn. But when the people were put outside, He went in and took her by the hand, and **the girl arose**" (verses 24–25 MEV, emphasis mine).

Jesus spoke the desired result—life not death, health not sickness. What happened? The girl was raised from the dead. We overcome by speaking in faith God's truth—what His Word says—not what the natural says it is. The girl was dead, but Jesus said she was asleep, and He woke her up. Your situation may appear "dead," hopeless or impossible, but do what Jesus did! Speak words of faith, words of victory, words of what you want the outcome to be.

The Blood of the Lamb Defeats the Accuser

The devil is not only a liar and a murderer; he's an accuser. Have you ever noticed that right after a major blessing or victory, along comes little, nagging doubts or accusations? Like "You didn't really get delivered... That prophecy she gave you is too good to be true... Do you remember last week when you did such and such...?"

Let's read Revelation chapter 12, verses 10–11, to see how to silence the accuser:

> Then I heard a loud voice saying in heaven, "Now salvation, and strength, and the kingdom of our God, and the power of His Christ have come, for the accuser of our brethren, who accused them before our God day and night, has been cast down. **And they overcame him by the blood of the Lamb and by the word of their testimony**, and they did not love their lives to the death." (NKJV – emphasis mine)

Look at the bolded words: "And they overcame him (the devil) by the blood of the Lamb and the word of their testimony." We've already talked about the importance of our testimony (of faith in Jesus) and the positive confession of our words lining up with what God says.

Jesus' blood is the foundation of our victory as overcomers. The devil cannot stand against the blood of Jesus. Satan was defeated at Calvary when the precious blood of Christ was shed for our redemption, salvation, healing, deliverance and everything else good.

The blood of Jesus is your number one weapon against Satan. Whenever he tries to steal your peace, rob you of your healing, deceive you out of your victory, or knock you over the head with yet another thing that's gone wrong... just let him know that Christ is in you, and He has already won the victory!

Rebuke the enemy, "Devil, I speak the blood of Jesus against you. Now, flee!" or "I apply the precious blood of Jesus to my (name the body part), and I am healed by His stripes." (See Isaiah 53:4–5, 1 Peter 2:24 and Matthew 8:17.)

Walk in the Love of God

The world's love is conditional, but there is never any offense in God's love. As Christ hung on the cross, battered and bruised, barely recognizable as a human being, He gazed down at the very ones who had spit on Him, mocked Him, and placed Him on that cross and said, "Father, forgive them for they know not what they do." His love bought our freedom. Can we do anything less? "Most important of all, continue to show deep love for each other, for love covers a multitude of sins" (1 Peter 4:8. NLT).

When asked by the rich young ruler which was the most important of God's commandments, "Jesus replied, 'You must love the Lord your God with all your heart, all your soul, and all your mind.' This is the first and greatest commandment. A second is equally important: 'Love your neighbor as yourself. The entire law and all the demands of the prophets are based on these two commandments'" (Matthew 22:37–40, NLT).

Jesus placed loving others on the same level as loving God! And in 1 John 4:20, the writer points out that we cannot love God whom we have not seen if we don't love our brother and sister whom we have seen.

What does this have to do with standing against your enemy? 1 John 4:8 says that "God is love." The devil cannot overcome God; therefore, he also cannot overcome you when you are walking in God's love. Where the presence of God is, no sickness, lack or evil work can exist!

Key Points

- God is on your side and He will fight your battles.
- Jesus overcame all worldly temptations for us.
- The blood of Jesus Christ is how we defeat Satan.
- Evil cannot stand against the love of God.
- Our words must line up with the Word of God.

Action Assignment:

God assures His people that He will fight for them. "The battle is not yours, but God's," says the word of the Lord in 2 Chronicles, chapter 20. The Israelites received a strange battle strategy after they released the attack they were facing to the Lord through fasting and prayer. Spend some time fasting (as the Lord leads you) and meditating on God's Word. You may also want to seek out a minister or mature believer who has experience with deliverance or healing ministry. Ask them to pray over you to bind the works of the enemy and cast out any spirits that have been harassing you. (See Matthew 18:18–20.)

Chapter 9

New Age, Demons and Angelic Intervention

The presence of evil and demonic spirit activity runs rampant in the world today, but if you know Jesus, you are protected, "...For this purpose the Son of God was manifested, that He might destroy the works of the devil" (1 John 3:8 NKJV).

Though we can't always see beyond this physical world, we know there is a spiritual realm—filled with both good and evil spirits. The popularity of New Age, or the occult, captivates many seeking supernatural power, activity and experiences.

New Age Philosophies and Practices

Séances, fortune-telling with tarot cards, palm reading or the like, horoscopes, hypnotism, Ouija boards, channeling, astral projection and other "paranormal" practices are not new. They have existed for thousands of years.

The Old Testament shares this warning, "Do not turn to spirits through mediums or necromancers. Do not seek after them to be defiled by them: I am the Lord your God" (Leviticus 19:31 MEV). Necromancers are those who practice black magic, witchcraft and communication with the dead through "familiar spirits." Astrology and horoscopes are also consulted by many today. Though they are seen as harmless fun or even when their guidance is taken seriously by some, these practices are condemned by God in the Bible.

Divination in the Old Testament

Examples of pagan "wisemen," magicians and astrologers are shown in the court of the Egyptian Pharaoh, who tried to refute God's supernatural signs demonstrated by Moses; also in Daniel, when King Nebuchadnezzar demanded that his "advisors" show him his dream and its meaning. These so-called wisemen and diviners could not do what the king asked and were sentenced to death. You probably know the story...enters in Daniel, after much prayer with his friends, who told the king his dream and its meaning, saving all of their lives. Daniel was filled with the Spirit of God, while these other men were operating out of the demonic spirit realm. There was no truth in them.

Daniel's interpretation of the prophetic message the king received in his dream proved true and came to pass throughout many centuries. The prophecies in the book of Daniel are still being fulfilled today and will culminate as believers look forward to the final days of man's government, the second coming of our Lord Jesus Christ, and the reign of His kingdom on earth.

Paul and the Fortune Teller

The apostles of the New Testament also came face-to-face with the occult. In Acts, chapter 16, *The Passion Translation* (TPT) tells the story,

> One day, as we were going to the house of prayer, we encountered a young slave girl who had an evil spirit of divination, the spirit of Python. [a] She had earned great profits for her owners by being a fortune-teller. She kept following us, shouting, "These men are servants of the Great High God, and they're telling us how to be saved!" Day after day she continued to do this, until Paul, greatly annoyed, turned and said to the spirit indwelling her, "I command you in the name of Jesus, the Anointed One, to come out of her, now!" At that very moment, the spirit came out of her! (verses 16–18)

---

[a] In the religious context of Greek mythology, she was an "oracle," a medium who had the spirit of the gods speaking through her to foretell the future. The Python spirit was the epithet of Apollo, known as the Greek god of prophecy. An individual (often a young virgin) who became the oracle of Apollo was known as the Python, or Pythia. (a footnote from The Passion Translation®. Copyright © 2017 by BroadStreet Publishing® Group, LLC. Used by permission. All rights reserved.)

Sorcery and Witchcraft Exposed

Other examples during the days of the Early Church are found in the book of Acts, such as when Paul confronted Bar-jesus (also called Elymus), the sorcerer, who tried to prevent Paul and Barnabas from witnessing to a high government official. (You can read the whole story in Acts, chapter 13.) And again, when Philip went down to Samaria and came upon a sorcerer named Simon, who used witchcraft and magic to deceive the people. (Read this story in its entirety in Acts, chapter 8.)

My Story

Years ago, before I came to know Jesus as my Savior and Lord, I was heavily involved in the occult. From tarot cards, astrology, Ouija boards and psychic phenomena to hypnotism, séances and astral projection, my like-minded friends and I were immersed in New Age practices. I had grown up in an unbelieving family and a very worldly and secular environment. Knowing nothing about God or the Bible, I had no idea I was actually serving the devil.

Praise God—He loves us no matter where we are in life. No matter what we've done, or failed to do, you and I can receive forgiveness and a brand-new, meaningful and blessed life in Jesus Christ. And, that's exactly what happened to me. God delivered me from those occult practices and everything else that was going on in my life that was contrary to His wonderful plans and purposes for me.

Worship the Creator, Not the Creation!

As believers in Christ Jesus, we worship the God who created the earth. New Age practices are idolatry, because they worship the creation, not the Creator. Today, these occultic influences and methods, sometimes masquerading as therapy, various treatments or "enlightened knowledge" are making their way into the fields of psychology, medicine and education in the forms of hypnosis, guided imagery or meditation, and emotion-numbing or stimulating prescription drugs.

Listen to this plainly spoken warning from *The Message* (MSG) Bible,

> Watch out for people who try to dazzle you with big words and intellectual double-talk. They want to drag you off into endless arguments that never amount to anything. They spread their ideas through the empty traditions of human beings and the empty superstitions of spirit beings. But that's not the way of Christ. Everything of God gets expressed in him, so you can see and hear him clearly. You don't need a telescope, a microscope, or a horoscope to realize the fullness of Christ, and the emptiness of the universe without him. When you come to him, that fullness comes together for you, too. His power extends over everything. (Colossians 2:8–10)

Believers Cast Out Devils

Yes, the power of Jesus extends over everything! Jesus gave His disciples authority in His Name and sent them out to witness to the people, heal the sick and set the captives free. After one such ministry trip, seventy of Jesus' "sent out ones" came back with this report, "...Lord, even the devils are subject unto us through thy name. And he said unto them, I beheld Satan as lightning fall from heaven" (Luke 10:17–18).

If you are a born-again believer, you have the power to cast out demons, too. This was not limited to the apostles or Early Church believers. I had such an experience in my own family. The Lord had blessed us with a newborn baby boy, who one day was unusually fussy and irritable. Nothing—not changing, feeding, rocking—nothing seemed to calm him down. The Holy Spirit revealed to me that the baby had recently been with a family member, who had been watching a violent murder-suicide and sexually-charged movie on TV while taking care of the baby.

This family member didn't know the Lord. They didn't understand how much what we see and hear can affect us, especially for a tiny, impressionable baby or child. Violence, illicit sex, witchcraft, profanity and rage pollute our society and are especially rampant on TV, the internet and social media. I took the baby and began to play songs about the blood of Jesus. I prayed over him and cast out the demonic and occultic spirits that were tormenting him. Praise God, within a short time, the baby was calm and smiling, and all fussiness was gone.

Satan Is Cast Out of Heaven

Jesus said the devil was cast out of heaven. Let's look at this account in Revelation, chapter 12, "And there was war in heaven: Michael and his angels fought against the dragon; and the dragon fought and his angels, and prevailed not; neither was their place found any more in heaven. And the great dragon was cast out, that old serpent, called the Devil, and Satan, which deceiveth the whole world: he was cast out into the earth, and his angels were cast out with him" (verses 7–9).

So now, Satan is walking the earth, like a roaring lion, seeking to devour the people of God (see 1 Peter 5:8). But, you don't need to fear! As Jesus gave authority to the seventy disciples, He gives authority over all demons to you and me today, "Behold, I give unto you power to tread on serpents and scorpions, and over all the power of the enemy: and nothing shall by any means hurt you" (Luke 10:19).

Jesus Triumphed Over Your Enemy

You may be going through difficult times or situations as the storms hit and try to beat you down. Stop! Re-focus your thoughts and trust in what Jesus did, "Then Jesus made a public spectacle of all the powers and principalities of darkness, stripping away from them every weapon and all their spiritual authority and power to accuse us. And by the power of the cross, Jesus led them around as prisoners in a procession of triumph. He was not their prisoner; they were his!" (Colossians 2:15 TPT)

You Have Power to Defeat the Enemy

The Christian walk requires daily growth and vigilance. As mentioned previously, we have an enemy, and just like a military army, we have been given weapons to fight our enemy:

> In conclusion, be strong in the Lord [draw your strength from Him and be empowered through your union with Him] and in the power of His [boundless] might. Put on the full armor of God [for His precepts are like the splendid armor of a heavily-armed soldier], so that you may be able to [successfully] stand up against all the schemes *and* the strategies *and* the deceits of the devil. For our struggle is not against flesh and blood [contending only with physical opponents], but against the rulers, against the powers, against the world forces of this [present] darkness, against the spiritual *forces* of wickedness in the heavenly (supernatural) *places*. (Ephesians 6:10–12 AMP)

Now that we've discovered who we're fighting—it's not people, but rather "the rulers, against the powers, against the world forces of this [present] darkness, against the spiritual forces of wickedness," let's read further and find out what weapons we have and how to use them!

Put On the Complete Armor of God and Stand Firm

Your heavenly armor will enable you to resist every attack of the enemy and to stand firm in your faith when it seems everything is crumbling around you. As you resist, stand, and hold your ground with your defensive armor, know that your victory is sure! You've stopped the attack of the enemy, and now you're ready to advance! Your offensive armor—the Word of God and prayer—will force the enemy to retreat and suffer defeat!

> Therefore, put on the complete armor of God, so that you will be able to [successfully] resist *and* stand your ground in the evil day [of danger], and having done everything [that the crisis demands], to stand firm [in your place, fully prepared, immovable, victorious]. So stand firm *and* hold your ground, HAVING TIGHTENED THE WIDE BAND OF TRUTH (personal integrity, moral courage) AROUND YOUR WAIST and HAVING PUT ON THE BREASTPLATE OF RIGHTEOUSNESS (an upright heart), and having strapped on YOUR FEET THE GOSPEL OF PEACE IN PREPARATION [to face the enemy with firm-footed stability and the readiness produced by the good news]. Above all, lift up the [protective] shield of faith with which you can extinguish all the flaming arrows of the evil *one*. And

> take THE HELMET OF SALVATION, and
> the sword of the Spirit, which is the Word
> of God. With all prayer and petition pray
> [with specific requests] at all times [on
> every occasion and in every season] in the
> Spirit, and with this in view, stay alert with
> all perseverance and petition [interceding
> in prayer] for all God's people. (Ephesians
> 6:13–18 AMP)

God will give you the victory! Be sure you stay vigilant and alert in the Spirit and prayer, and remember, we are an army of believers. You and I must enforce the victory that Christ won, not only for ourselves and our loved ones, but for all believers in the Body of Christ.

The world has a saying these days, "Better together." Nowhere is that more important than in the Church…"A new commandment I give unto you, That ye love one another; as I have loved you, that ye also love one another. By this shall all men know that ye are my disciples, if ye have love one to another" (John 13:34–35).

Angelic Intervention

I've had encounters with both demons and angels. My spiritual eyes have been opened to see into the spirit realm a few times where demons were present, usually to warn of some impending danger. I've also seen demons while praying for people that were oppressed or controlled by evil spirits. God gave me understanding so that I could cast out the demons (see Mark 16:17).

I remember one time at a church in Orlando, Florida, where the gifts of the Holy Spirit and many supernatural manifestations occurred frequently, seeing in the Spirit two angels outside of the church stationed at the entryway to the property. They looked like warriors with swords ready to draw at a moment's notice should danger arise. The angels were huge (at least two stories high), majestic-looking, and were faithfully guarding the church and all of its grounds. People drove in and out and walked about, totally unaware of the angels' presence.

Messenger and Warning Angels

I love angel stories! In the Bible, we see how God used angels to bring messages to people, such as in the story of the virgin Mary, as well as warnings such as was given to Balaam in Numbers, chapter 22, where the Lord's anger was kindled against him for conspiring with the enemies of the Israelites. There are many examples in God's Word where angels delivered messages from the Lord or intervened in the affairs of man.

Cities and Nations Have Ruling Spirits

In Daniel, chapter 10, Daniel was praying for under-standing about the future of his people, who were in captivity. God sent the angel, Gabriel, in answer to Daniel's prayer, but it took 21 days for him to get to Daniel. Why? There was war in the heavenlies between Satan's territorial spirits and God's angels. This shows that cities and nations have ruling spirits over them that influence government, culture and the lives of their citizens. Sometimes, you will see cities where certain spirits are prevalent, like crime in Chicago, gambling in Las Vegas, and promiscuity in Hollywood.

An Angel Brings Revelation and Breakthrough

When Gabriel finally broke through the demon princes, he said to Daniel, "Now I am here to tell you what will happen to your people, the Jews, at the end times—for the fulfillment of this prophecy is many years away" (verse 14 TLB). This archangel was sent to Daniel to reveal the things to come in answer to Daniel's prayer and fasting. So here, we see angelic intervention bringing prophetic revelation and breakthrough.

Angels Are Assigned to Protect Those Who Obey God

In Psalm 91, which we discussed in an earlier chapter, we saw that God gave angels the assignment to protect those who dwelled in the secret place of God; in other words, they had an intimate relationship with God and obeyed His Word. Do you have an angel? Yes! "Are not all the angels ministering spirits sent out [by God] to serve (accompany, protect) those who will inherit salvation? [Of course they are!]" (Hebrews 1:14 AMP)

Guardian and Guiding Angels

You do not have to worry about the safety of your children. Jesus taught, "Beware that you don't look down upon a single one of these little children. For I tell you that in heaven their angels have constant access to my Father" (Matthew 18:10 TLB). It is commonly believed that all children have guardian angels; however, some Bible versions translate "children" as "little ones" or in *The Message* (MSG) translation as "childlike believers."

The Israelites were delivered from Egypt and on their way to the Promised Land. God spoke to them about the angel He had commanded to protect them, guide them, and bring them safely into the place, the plan and the promise He had for them, "Behold, I send an Angel before you to keep you in the way and to bring you into the place which I have prepared" (Exodus 23:20 NKJV).

Even today, God may use angels to bring about His plans and purposes in our lives, though we have a better covenant than did the people of the Old Testament. We have Jesus (our good Shepherd, whose voice we hear and follow). We have God's Word to guide and guard us each day. And, we have the Holy Spirit to tell us all things, as Jesus foretold, and to lead us into all truth.

Angels to the Rescue

Another favorite angel scripture is this: "The angel of the Lord encamps around those who fear Him [with awe-inspired reverence and worship Him with obedience], And He rescues [each of] them" (Psalm 34:7).

Think back to times where you were protected supernaturally—You had no idea how you escaped danger or maybe even a deadly accident, but at the last second, "something" intervened and saved you. It could have been an angel!

Angels can appear in different forms. Satan can transform himself into an angel of light (see 2 Corinthians 11:14). Angels can take on the appearance of normal human beings. Hebrews 13:1–2 says, "Let brotherly love continue. Be not forgetful to entertain strangers: for thereby some have entertained angels unawares.

As we draw close to the Lord, worship Him, and obey His Word, we can have the assurance that there are angels all around us to do the bidding of a loving and watchful God. "Praise the Lord, you his angels, you mighty ones who do his bidding, who obey his word" (Psalm 103:20 NIV).

Key Points
- New Age philosophies and practices can open the door to the devil.
- Worship the Creator, not the creation.
- You have supernatural weapons—Put on the armor of God.
- Angels bring messages and warnings, protection and deliverance.
- Angels can appear in various forms, and we may not recognize them.

Action Assignment:
Ask the Holy Spirit to reveal to you anything from your past or present that is inviting demonic activity into your life or home. If you are or have been involved with any occultic practice or teaching or associate with people who are involved in New Age, Eastern religions, or other demonic activity, get these things out of your life fast! Repent, renounce any soul ties, generational curses or witchcraft spells that have been spoken against you. (The next chapter will help with this.)

Chapter 10

How to Rid Your Home
of Uninvited Demonic Guests

By Kathy DeGraw

In this chapter, I'd like to share an article by Kathy DeGraw that I think gives insight into the demonic influences that sometimes infiltrate families and homes, even those of believers. At the end of this article, I am going to share how you, as a Christ-follower, have the power through the Holy Spirit to wage spiritual warfare against the devil—and win! Here is Kathy's article…

(Reprinted with permission from *Charisma*. Copyright © 2017 by Charisma Media, USA. All rights reserved. *www.charismamag.com*)

Demons can infiltrate our homes, release spiritual warfare attacks and have us feeling heaviness, burdened and depressed. Uninvited demonic guests coming into our home can create stagnancy in our spiritual walk and emotional paralysis.

Demons Can Enter in the Following Ways:
- Television
- Music
- New items purchased
- Territorial spirits: local or traveling
- Familiar spirits: regional or family spirits
- Object attachments
- Arguments
- Sickness
- Disunity
- Friends, relatives, visitors
- Prior occupancy and establishment

It is important to keep our home spiritually clean. Spiritually cleaning our home will prevent future spiritual warfare attacks and will create an environment conducive for a move of the Holy Spirit.

Now that demons have infiltrated your home, how do you get rid of them?

The following are steps to spiritually clean your home:
1. Play Christian music 24/7. Music is declarations and includes scriptures. Make sure the Christian music witnesses in your spirit man and does not agitate you. Not all Christian music is as Christian and holy as it should be.
2. Play scriptures or read scriptures out loud in your home. Rotate between worship music and having the Bible read out loud through your media device.

3. Pray through and anoint each room. Anoint your doorposts and entry and exits. Anoint each room and consecrate it unto the Lord. Speak that it will exude the presence of the Lord and that the atmosphere will establish peace for all who enter.

Pray Specifically Over Each Room

- **Bedrooms:** Command all spirits of lust, perversion and masturbation to leave. Command and pray out loud that demons will not release tormenting dreams, nightmares or incubus or succubus spirits in the night. Speak and decree that your sleep will be sweet.

- **Bathrooms:** Bind and restrict sickness, disease, upset stomachs and intestinal issues. Command everyone's colon, digestive system and intestines to work properly in Jesus' Name. Command spirits of self-hate, self-rejection, vanity and pride to go in Jesus' Name. Call forth as people look in the mirror that they will see themselves made in the image of God and feel His great love for them.

- **Kitchen:** Speak and decree there will be no food poisoning. Come against sickness and disease and the spirits of obesity, anorexia, gluttony, overeating and weight problems. Pray further and bind the spirit of addiction including alcoholism, caffeine, sugar and other food addictions. Bind and restrict emotional ailments and call forth inner healing for all who enter the kitchen that their emotional challenges, feelings

119

of unworthiness, and stress will not cause them to find comfort in food.

- **Dining Room:** Cast out a spirit of dissension and disunity. Call forth good family relationships where the love of God abounds. Pray conversations would be edifying and glorify the Lord while eating at the table.

- **Living Room / Family Room:** Cast out every demon that has infiltrated through TV shows, vulgar language and computer pornography. Bind and restrict a spirit of electronic addiction. Play Christian music in this room to permeate the atmosphere. Even if not watching what you would consider terrible shows, many demons infiltrate through a variety of shows released into the atmosphere of your home.

- **Furnace Room:** Pray against demonic infiltration. Prior families who have lived there may have deposited unknowingly demonic influences. Demons often hide out in the furnace and infiltrate the house through the venting system. Anoint the furnace with oil and command all demons to go in Jesus' Name.

- **Storage Room:** Be alert and aware of items brought back from traveling such as luggage. Demons can attach to objects from other regions and wreak havoc on your home. Items stored for a long period, given as gifts, or family items passed down from generations can all have demonic attachments.

Pray Specifically Concerning Visitors or Guests

- Pray after people leave your home that do not have a walk glorifying the Lord or that you feel deposited a spirit of heaviness. Sometimes people leave, and we feel agitated or less joy. You may feel weighted, all of a sudden depressed or frustrated with your time together. Say out loud and pray, "I command there will be no ungodly attachments, defilements or transferences in Jesus' Name. I bind and restrict every ungodly soul tie and say you will not activate and implant in Jesus' Name."

Now that you prayed through your home and have done a spiritual cleansing, how can you prevent your home from receiving future demonic infiltrations?

The following steps are not to be legalistic but can help dedicate your home unto the Lord.

- Write scripture on the walls and floors before painting and carpeting.
- Anoint each room with oil.
- Write scriptures on your entry doorposts.
- Play music or scriptures throughout your home, even while at work, and keep on a low volume in another room at night.
- Stake out your home. Write scriptures on four stakes and pound completely into the dirt at the four corners of your property.
- Do a prayer walk around the inside and outside of your home.

These practices are not superstitious, paranoid or legalistic. They are creating a peaceful environment and stating that your home is built on the foundation of Jesus Christ, and you are dedicating and consecrating your home unto the Lord. ❧

Kathy DeGraw is a prophetic deliverance minister. She is the founder of Kathy DeGraw Ministries and Be Love Outreach. She is the author of several books including; Speak Out, Discerning and Destroying the Works of Satan, Identity Invasion, Who is Speaking? and Warfare Declarations. Visit https://www.degrawministries.org/ to learn more about Kathy.

You Are Seated with Christ in Heavenly Places

As a born-again believer, you have an exalted place that Satan can't touch because you have dominion over him. Where is this place and what do you have there? Ephesians chapter 1, verse 3, says, "Blessed be the God and Father of our Lord Jesus Christ, who hath blessed us with **all spiritual blessings** in **heavenly places in Christ**…" And, Ephesians 2:6 makes it even clearer, "and hath **raised us up together, and made us sit together in heavenly places in Christ Jesus**…(emphasis mine)"

God Has Given You Spiritual Power Over Satan

…and what is the exceeding greatness of his
power to us-ward who believe, according

to the working of his mighty power, which he wrought in Christ, when he raised him from the dead, and set him at his own right hand **in the heavenly places, far above all principality, and power, and might, and dominion**, and every name that is named, not only in this world, but also in that which is to come: and hath put all things under his feet, and gave him to be the head over all things to the church, which is his body, the fulness of him that filleth all in all. (Ephesians 1:19–23)

Because we are seated in heavenly places with Christ Jesus, we are above **all** principalities and powers. These are multiple levels of demons that have been sent to harass, trick, tempt, and try to destroy you, your family, and God's plan for your lives. But, as I already declared, the devil can't touch you. Jesus Christ defeated him once and for all on the cross.

The devil can try to make you believe he has power, but it's a lie. Satan has no power over a believer. He is under your feet. I like the way *The Passion Translation* puts it, "And the God of peace will swiftly pound Satan to a pulp under your feet! And the wonderful favor of our Lord Jesus will surround you" (Romans 16:20 TPT).

Spiritual Warfare in the End Times
In these last days, there is an increase in witchcraft and other demonic activity of the occult. (See also chapter 9.)

Evil and darkness will continue to escalate at a rapid pace. Yet, there will be greater revival and supernatural power in the Church as the return of Jesus draws near, and the devil will not be able to overcome it. Jesus prophesied in Matthew 16:18, "I will build my church; and the gates of hell shall not prevail against it."

You are part of the Body of Christ, which is the Church. And just as Satan will not prevail against the Church, he cannot prevail against you. One very important thing I've learned about dealing with the devil is "DO NOT FEAR!" When demons rear their ugly heads, know that greater is He (Jesus) that is in you than he (the devil) that is in the world (see 1 John 4:4) and that God has not given you the spirit of fear (see 2 Timothy 1:7). Just as faith opens the door to God—fear, which is the opposite of faith, will open the door to the devil.

Walk in the Holy Spirit
and Overcome the Works of the Flesh

No principality or power has any authority over you, "But if ye be led of the Spirit, ye are not under the law" (Galatians 5:18). Paul goes on in verses 19–21 to list the works of the flesh over which God has given us power if we are led by His Spirit… "Now the practices of the sinful nature are *clearly* evident: they are sexual immorality, impurity, sensuality (total irresponsibility, lack of self-control), idolatry, sorcery, hostility, strife, jealousy, fits of anger, disputes, dissensions, factions [that promote heresies], envy, drunkenness, riotous behavior, and *other* things like these" (AMP).

You have power over witchcraft, sorcery—and all the spirits of darkness and evil—if you are led by the Spirit of God. The power of the Holy Spirit is so much greater than anything in this world that is under the control of Satan. Dare to take your place with Christ in heavenly places and enforce your God-given authority now to bind the devil, **"Satan, I bind you from...(name areas in your life where you are having spiritual battles), and I loose the power of the Holy Spirit to (speak the desired outcome). In Jesus' Name, Amen."**

Key Points

- You are seated with Christ in heavenly places.
- God has given you spiritual power over Satan.
- If you are a born-again believer, Satan can't touch you.
- Christ has defeated the devil once and for all on the cross.
- You can overcome the works of the flesh in the Spirit.

Action Assignment:
If the Lord has revealed to you that demons or curses have infiltrated your mind, health, family, home, or other area of your life, follow the instructions in this chapter. Read also 2 Timothy 1:7, 1 John 4:4 and Luke 10:19. Do not allow fear or intimidation to grab hold of you because God has not given you the spirit of fear, but of power, love and a sound mind (see 2 Timothy 1:7). Remember that greater is He (Jesus) in you than he (the devil) that is in the world (see 1 John 4:4), and that Jesus has given you power over all the works of the enemy (see Luke 10:19).

Chapter 11

Not by Might

In an earlier chapter, we talked about how Jesus is our example in discovering the strategies needed to overcome Satan's attacks. We also learned that when Jesus ascended from earth to heaven to sit at the right hand of His Father's throne, He left us another Comforter and Helper, the Holy Spirit. "But when the truth-giving Spirit comes, he will unveil the reality of every truth within you. He won't speak his own message, but only what he hears from the Father, and he will reveal prophetically to you what is to come" (John 16:13 TPT).

We can see from the Scriptures that the Holy Spirit has come to comfort, help, and reveal truth—present truth and prophetic truth—that which is to come in the future. Jesus is telling this to His disciples, then and now, because His message is for today's believers, too.

The Holy Spirit Has Come
"And when he comes, he will convict the world of

its sin, and of God's righteousness, and of the coming judgment. The world's sin is that it refuses to believe in me. Righteousness is available because I go to the Father, and you will see me no more. Judgment will come because the ruler of this world has already been judged" (John 16:8–11 NLT).

Another facet of the ministry of the Holy Spirit is to guide the people of God corporately in the Church as well as in our own individual lives. It is wisdom that we don't make decisions and take action based only on our own human intellect, but to wait on the Lord, praying and listening for the voice of God's Spirit. He helps us to pray according to God's will, "And the Holy Spirit helps us in our weakness. For example, we don't know what God wants us to pray for. But the Holy Spirit prays for us with groanings that cannot be expressed in words" (Romans 8:26 NLT).

I Just Can't Do It

There are many things in the Christian life that may seem difficult, if not downright impossible, such as being obedient, doing the right thing, always loving, forgiving, putting the needs of others before our own…the list goes on. We cannot live the Christian life and fulfill the ministry God has ordained for each of us with our own ability and in our own strength. And, the good news is that God doesn't expect us to…

> Then he said to me, "This is what the Lord
> says to Zerubbabel: It is not by force nor by

strength, but by my Spirit, says the Lord of
Heaven's Armies. (Zechariah 4:6 NLT)

Take courage when you are about to undertake
something new that in the natural seems impossible. It
may be a responsibility given to you that has completely
overwhelmed you or for which you feel totally inadequate.
It may just be the ordinary tasks of daily life, which
sometimes become too much to cope with in an already
overburdened schedule. It may be a decision you need to
make, and you don't know which way to turn. A friend
may ask you to pray, but you don't know where to begin.
The Holy Spirit is here to help!

A Great Multitude of Armies
Set Out to Invade Israel and Judah

Briefly mentioned previously, let's go into more depth
in the story from 2 Chronicles, chapter 20, in the *Modern
English Version...*

The armies of Israel and Judah were vastly outnumbered
as a "large multitude" from Ammon, Moab, and Mount Seir
were en route to invade God's people. "Jehoshaphat was
fearful and set himself to seek the LORD" (verses 1, 3). The
king and his people prayed and fasted, and said to the LORD,
"… For we have not strength enough to stand before this
great army that is coming against us. And we do not know
what we should do, but our eyes are on You" (verse 12).

The Spirit of the LORD came on a prophet in their
midst. "And he said, 'Pay attention all Judah, and those
dwelling in Jerusalem, and King Jehoshaphat: Thus says

the LORD to you, 'Do not fear, nor be dismayed because of this great army, for the battle is not yours, but God's. Tomorrow, go down against them…It will not be necessary for you to fight in this conflict. Take your positions, stand, and observe the deliverance of the LORD for you, O Judah and Jerusalem.' Do not fear or be filled with terror. Tomorrow, go out before them, and the LORD will be with you'" (verses 15–17).

Holy Spirit's Creative Battle Strategy

Normal operations would likely be to attack the enemy by surprise or maybe head-on in plain view, however the military leader commanded, but in this battle, the Spirit of God took over. "So they rose up early in the morning and went out to the Wilderness of Tekoa. And he consulted with the people and then appointed singers for the LORD and those praising Him in holy attire as they went before those equipped for battle saying, 'Praise the LORD, for His mercy endures forever'" (verses 20–21).

What? Who ever heard of sending a choir before the army of fighting men? Surely, there will be hundreds or thousands of casualties! But, here's what happened… "When they began singing and praising, the LORD set ambushes against Ammon, Moab, and Mount Seir, who had come against Judah; so they were defeated" (verse 22).

Praise God! By natural means, this could never have happened. God's people were outnumbered and would never have stood a chance to defeat the strong, opposing armies that had threatened to wipe them out.

Midnight Praise Delivers the Apostles

Another example where the Holy Spirit delivered God's people through praise is found in the book of Acts. The apostles, Paul and Silas, had been thrown into prison. Now, most people dragged off unlawfully by the local officials would have been really angry to say the least. Not Paul and Silas...look at the Lord-honoring attitude they displayed there in that dirty, rat-infested cell where they were bound after being brutally beaten.

> But about midnight when **Paul and Silas were praying and singing hymns of praise to God**, and the prisoners were listening to them; suddenly there was a great earthquake, so [powerful] that **the very foundations of the prison were shaken and at once all the doors were opened and everyone's chains were unfastened**. When the jailer, shaken out of sleep, saw the prison doors open, he drew his sword and was about to kill himself, thinking that the prisoners had escaped. But Paul shouted, saying, "Do not hurt yourself, we are all here! (Acts 16:25–28 AMP – emphasis mine)

God inhabits the praises of His people. The Holy Spirit, in response to the faith, prayers and praise of Paul and Silas, did what man could not do. He opened the prison doors. It may have appeared to be a natural phenomenon (an earthquake), but it was truly the work of God's Spirit.

God uses every opportunity to show His love and grace to people. Look what happened next.

The Jailer and His Family Are Saved

> Then the jailer called for torches and rushed in, and trembling with fear he fell down before Paul and Silas, and after he brought them out [of the inner prison], he said, "Sirs, what must I do to be saved?" And they answered, "Believe in the Lord Jesus [as your personal Savior and entrust yourself to Him] and you will be saved, you and your household [if they also believe]." And they spoke the word of the Lord [concerning eternal salvation through faith in Christ] to him and to all who were in his house. And he took them that very hour of the night and washed their bloody wounds, and immediately he was baptized, he and all his household. Then he brought them into his house and set food before them, and rejoiced greatly, since he had believed in God with his entire family [accepting with joy what had been made known to them about the Christ]. (Acts 16:29–34 AMP)

Supernatural Favor and Protection

Friend, next time you find yourself facing an "impossible" situation, call on the Holy Spirit. Learn to recognize His voice. He will guide you. He will give you favor and supernaturally arrange people, places and things to bring you victory. His strategy may seem unusual or even foolish sometimes, but God's ways always work!

Remember, our praise gives the Holy Spirit an open door into our lives. Praise draws God to us—and invites His intervention in the concerns and needs we have lifted up to Him in prayer. In the Bible, the book of Ezra declares that "...Our God's hand of protection is on all who worship him..." (verse 8:22 NLT).

"Not by might, not by power, but by My Spirit says the Lord" (Zechariah 4:6)...Just as you are pleased when your children look to you for comfort, protection, advice and help, so is our Heavenly Father pleased when (sometimes after exhausting our own human intellect and futile efforts), we finally turn to Him, humbly admitting we can't do it on our own, but we need the power of the Holy Spirit.

Dr. Bruce Wilkinson, author of the best-selling book, *The Prayer of Jabez*, which has sold over nine-million copies since its release, shares a personal experience in his book on the lesson of trusting the Father and not relying upon ourselves:

A Ladder to the Clouds

One day when our kids were preschoolers, Darlene and I found ourselves with them at a large city park in southern California. It was the kind of park that makes a grown man wish he were a kid again. It had swings, monkey bars, and seesaws, but what was most enticing were the slides— not just one slide, but three—from small, to medium, to enormous. David, who was five at the time, took off like a shot for the small slide.

"Why don't you go down with him?" Darlene suggested. But I had another idea. "Let's wait and see what happens," I said. So we relaxed on a nearby bench and watched. David clambered happily to the top of the smallest slide. He waved over at us with a big smile, then whizzed down.

Without hesitation he moved over to the medium-sized slide. He had climbed halfway up the ladder when he turned and looked at me. I looked away. He pondered his options for a moment, then carefully backed down one step at a time. "Honey, you ought to go help him out," my wife said. "Not yet," I replied, hoping the twinkle in my eye would reassure her that I wasn't just being careless.

David spent a few minutes at the bottom of the middle slide watching other kids climb up, whiz down, and run around to do it again. Finally his little mind was made up. He could do it. He climbed up...and slid down. Three times, in fact, without even looking at us.

Then we watched him turn and head toward the highest slide. Now Darlene was getting anxious. "Bruce, I don't think he should do that by himself, do you?"

"No," I replied as calmly as possible. "But I don't think he will. Let's see what he does." When David reached the bottom of the giant slide, he turned and called out, "Daddy!" But I glanced away again, pretending I couldn't hear him.

He peered up the ladder. In his young imagination, it must have reached to the clouds. He watched a teenage boy go hurtling down the slide. Then, against all odds, he decided to try. Step-by-step, hand over hand, he inched up the ladder. He hadn't reached a third of the way when he froze. By this time, the teenager was coming up behind him and yelled at him to get going. But David couldn't. He couldn't go up or down. He had reached the point of certain failure.

I rushed over. "Are you okay, son?" I asked from the bottom of the ladder. He looked down at me, shaken but clinging to that ladder with steely determination. And I could tell he had a question ready. "Dad, will you come down the slide with me?" he asked. The teenager was losing patience, but I wasn't about to let the moment go.

"Why son?" I asked, peering up into his little face. "I can't do it without you, Dad," he said, trembling. "It's too big for me!" I stretched as high as I could to reach him and lifted him into my arms. Then we climbed that long ladder up to the clouds together. At the top, I put my son between my legs and wrapped my arms around him. Then we went zipping down the slide together, laughing all the way."

His Hand, His Spirit

That is what your Father's hand is like. You tell Him, "Father, please do this in me because I can't do it alone! It's too big for me!" And you step out in faith to say and do things that could only come from His hand. Afterwards, your spirit is shouting, God did that, nobody else! God carried me, gave me the words, gave me the power—and it is wonderful! *(Excerpted from The Prayer of Jabez© by Exponential, Inc. Used by permission of WaterBrook*

Multnomah Publishing Group, a division of Random House, Inc.)

Key Points
- God doesn't expect us to live the Christian life on our own.
- Jesus left us another Comforter and Helper, the Holy Spirit.
- The Holy Spirit can do what man cannot do.
- The Word says, "It's not by might, nor by power, but by My Spirit."
- Our praise gives the Holy Spirit an open door into our lives.

Action Assignment:
Ephesians 3:20 (AMP) says, "Now to Him who is able to [carry out His purpose and] do superabundantly more than all that we dare ask or think [infinitely beyond our greatest prayers, hopes, or dreams], according to His power that is at work within us," Take some time to think about and write down in your journal how you may be limiting God from accomplishing all He wants for you. Read Isaiah 55:8–9. Then say, "Lord, I repent over putting You in a box and trying to do things my way by my own strength and abilities, which I now realize are inferior to Your ways. I commit this situation (name it) to You. You alone are my Source, and I trust You to bring the answer."

Chapter 12

Supernatural Strategies

We are living in strategic, critical times where people may no longer be able to turn to the things they have depended on for support and safety in the past. There may come a time when hospitals are not available, government assistance is not available, and "business as usual" will not meet their needs. Both Christian and secular authorities have warned that the United States' electrical grid is a prime target for enemy nations to launch an EMP attack that would kill many and cause the nation to regress back into "pioneer" days. Electricity, technology, transportation and other things we've come to regard as necessities would come to a grinding halt. Food, gas and other commodities would be in short supply. Looters would be a constant threat to safety and security.

A Deadly Scenario

An EMP attack would be just one possible deadly scenario. Others include nuclear incidents, biological or chemical attacks, incurable plagues or natural disasters, possible civil war or martial law developing out of division, revolution or violence in the streets of America. These are very real perils, "This know also, that in the last days perilous times shall come" (2 Timothy 3:1).

Believers and unbelievers alike will have to learn to trust God for their very survival. (For more information, please read my book, *The Answer Book for Troubled Times*, available on Amazon, Barnes & Noble.com, Google Play, or on my website, HealingforAmerica.com.)

The Plans of the Spirit Are
Birthed into this Realm through Prayer

"I learned a long time ago that the plans of the Spirit are birthed into this realm through prayer. God's Word is forever settled in heaven but must be established on earth. We, as a people, must pray out the plan of God to be established on the earth. We must take authority over the demonic spirits and curses through prayer. When we pray, God exposes the deceitful strategies of the enemy and makes a way for His purposes to be established," asserts Faisal Malick, author, speaker, TV host and former Muslim-turned-Christ-follower, in chapter 8 of *The Answer Book for Troubled Times*.

God's purposes include your healing, financial breakthrough, family members being saved and walking in God's will, and anything else you're believing for from God. Jesus came to set us free from sin, sickness (including coronavirus and other pandemics or plagues), and every demonic curse.

"The Spirit of the Lord is on me, because he has anointed me to preach good news to the poor. He has sent me to proclaim freedom for the prisoners and recovery of sight for the blind, to release the oppressed, to proclaim the year of the Lord's favor." (Luke 4:18–19, NIV)

"Be It unto You According to Your Faith"

When Jesus walked the earth, He did many miracles of provision, healing, deliverance and even raising the dead! More often than not, you would hear Him say, "Be it unto you according to your faith."

If I had to choose the top key to kingdom living, I would pick FAITH, without a doubt. Friend, I encourage you to raise the level of your faith. How? By believing the Word of God. The Bible says that if all the works of Jesus were to be recorded, the whole world couldn't hold the books that would be written. Let's look at just a couple of the miracles Jesus did, His disciples did, and you and I, as believers, can do…

Practical, Everyday Needs
Meet the Miraculous Hand of God!

In both the Old and New Testaments there are many miracles from parting the Red Sea to walking on water. In these troubled times, we will need the kind of faith that moved the prophets and patriarchs of old as well as the followers of Jesus to believe that "all things are possible with God!"

And Jesus went forth, and saw a great multitude, and was moved with compassion toward them, and he healed their sick. And when it was evening, his disciples came to him, saying, This is a desert place, and the time is now past; send the multitude away, that they may go into the villages, and buy themselves victuals. But Jesus said unto them, They need not depart; give ye them to eat. And they say unto him, We have here but five loaves, and two fishes. He said, Bring them hither to me. And he commanded the multitude to sit down on the grass, and took the five loaves, and the two fishes, and looking up to heaven, he blessed, and brake, and gave the loaves to his disciples, and the disciples to the multitude. And they did all eat, and were filled: and they took up of the fragments that remained twelve baskets full. And they that had eaten were about five thousand men, beside women and children. (Matthew 14:14–21)

The Love and Compassion of God Never Fails

Jesus demonstrated the love and compassion of God through the incredible miracles He performed in the lives of anyone who would believe He was the Son of God! Jesus healed the sick and set the captives free everywhere He traveled. "How God anointed and consecrated Jesus of Nazareth with the [Holy] Spirit and with strength and ability and power; how He went about doing good and, in particular, **curing all** who were harassed and oppressed by [the power of] the devil, for God was with Him" (Acts 10:38, AMP – emphasis mine).

Notice, the scripture says "curing all"—**Jesus never turned away anyone who had faith to believe.** So, be confident today that whatever you are facing, whether it be a health problem, a family or relationship that needs fixing, or a financial need, it is God's will to heal you, and to bring provision, hope and restoration.

It Is God's Will to Heal You

My friend, when you are asking God for your healing or victory, you must have steadfast, unshakeable faith that Jesus heals today just like He did in Bible times. **Jesus *is* willing to heal and deliver you.**

> Suddenly, a man with leprosy approached him and knelt before him. "Lord," the man said, "if you are willing, you can heal me and make me clean." Jesus reached out and touched him. "I am willing," he said. "Be healed!" And instantly the leprosy disappeared. (Matthew 8:2–3, NLT)

Are you wondering how you are going to pay your bills? Or pay for your children's education? Jesus took care of Peter's tax debt and His own in a supernatural way that defied the laws of nature and human comprehension. Jesus told Peter to go fishing, which was his life trade, and to open the mouth of the first fish he caught. In the fish's mouth, Peter found two coins, enough to pay both Jesus' and his own taxes. (You can read this story in Matthew 17:24–27.)

Jesus' Ways of Meeting Your Need Are Limitless

Jesus can bring supernatural provision for you too when you are wondering, "How am I ever going to make ends meet?" Jesus may not send you fishing, but His ways are limitless, surpassing man's ingenuity and ability. When you ask God for financial or other provision, be sure not to "box" Him in with your own limited understanding!

Be open to unusual, creative strategies, and supernatural miracles, that God will use to take care of your need. When you hear His voice, which will always agree with His Word, follow whatever direction He gives you, and watch Him work powerfully in your behalf. Praise the Lord for His goodness and mercy, and expect good things, not bad things to happen. God will come through for you if you trust and do not doubt! "For with God nothing is ever impossible and no word from God shall be without power or impossible of fulfillment" (Luke 1:37 AMP).

Watch Your Words

Your words must line up with the Word of God! Faith and power words go together—This unbeatable combination activates miracles, signs and wonders! Refuse to allow yourself to believe and speak the worst! What you say is vital to receiving your healing, your miracle provision, or anything else in this supernatural kingdom life. The Bible says that "out of the abundance of the heart, the mouth speaks." What you believe in your heart will eventually come out in what you say and affect the corresponding action you take—good or bad.

Numerous scriptures show the importance of keeping your words (and your heart) lined up with the Word of God. "The tongue can bring death or life; those who love to talk will reap the consequences" (Proverbs 18:21 NLT). After demonstrating the power of His words on a fig tree that didn't bear fruit (Mark 11:12–14, 20–21), Jesus taught His disciples,

> ...Have faith in God [constantly]. Truly I tell you, whoever says to this mountain, Be lifted up and thrown into the sea! and **does not doubt at all in his heart but believes that what he says will take place**, it will be done for him. For this reason I am telling you, whatever you ask for in prayer, believe (trust and be confident) that it is granted to you, and you will [get it]. **And whenever you stand praying, if you have anything against anyone, forgive him and let it drop (leave it, let it go), in order that your Father Who is in heaven may also forgive you your [own] failings and shortcomings and let them drop.** (Mark 11:22–25 AMP – emphasis mine)

Notice the emphasis in this portion of scripture. The right words will come out of a heart filled with unshakeable faith! Understand this, faith in your heart is not active and productive until it is spoken and acted upon.

Overcoming Every Enemy Attack

I would like to take just a moment here to point out the last verse, which shows the tremendous importance of making sure our hearts are right before God, particularly in the area of forgiveness. If we are holding something against someone, especially husbands and wives (see 1 Peter 3:8), but really it applies to everyone; our prayers will be hindered. The answers to prayer that we are seeking, will not come until we make things right with God and with others.

God is love, the Master of forgiveness, and He expects us to walk in love toward our enemies. In fact, walking in God's ways of love and forgiveness can neutralize every attack against you. "When a man's ways please the Lord, He makes even his enemies to be at peace with him" (Proverbs 16:7 NKJV).

The Disciples Heal a Cripple in Jesus' Name

Here's a man, who didn't know anything about Jesus, as far as we know from the scriptures below. He didn't have faith. He didn't ask to be healed. He was just looking for a handout, but he got far more!

> Now Peter and John went up together into the temple at the hour of prayer, being the ninth hour. And a certain man lame from his mother's womb was carried, whom

they laid daily at the gate of the temple which is called Beautiful, to ask alms of them that entered into the temple; who seeing Peter and John about to go into the temple asked an alms. And Peter, fastening his eyes upon him with John, said, Look on us. And he gave heed unto them, expecting to receive something of them. Then Peter said, Silver and gold have I none; but such as I have give I thee: In the name of Jesus Christ of Nazareth rise up and walk. And he took him by the right hand, and lifted him up: and immediately his feet and ankle bones received strength. And he leaping up stood, and walked, and entered with them into the temple, walking, and leaping, and praising God. And all the people saw him walking and praising God: and they knew that it was he which sat for alms at the Beautiful gate of the temple: and they were filled with wonder and amazement at that which had happened unto him. (Acts 3:1–10)

The Power of God Is in You

Jesus performed many healings and miracles during the brief time He walked on this earth. He imparted His teachings and anointing to His disciples. Before Jesus left to be with His Father in heaven, He offered a prayer (see John 17) for His disciples and all that would follow, including you and me. "Just as You commissioned and sent Me into the world, I also have commissioned and sent them (believers) into the world" (John 17:18 AMP). You and I are called to go into the harvest field...to share the gospel and heal the sick. (See Matthew 28:19, John 14:12.)

Through God's miracle-working power, you can overcome danger, and rise above natural circumstances. If you are walking in the kingdom life God has planned for you, here is what you can do when you believe.

> And these signs will follow those who believe: In My name they will cast out demons; they will speak with new tongues; they will take up serpents; and if they drink anything deadly, it will by no means hurt them; they will lay hands on the sick, and (the sick) will recover... And they went out and preached everywhere, the Lord working with them and confirming the word through the accompanying signs. (Mark 16:17–18, 20 NKJV)

Faith, salvation in Christ, knowing and speaking God's Word, hearing and obeying the Holy Spirit and the wisdom of God... These are the spiritual essentials for victory in your life, and they all work together. For example, you can't speak the Word of God unless you know it, and you can't expect to see results if your words are not spoken from a heart of faith.

Sometimes, when a problem arises, we start spouting out scriptures and wonder why they don't seem to work even though we are believing in faith. We must ask God for His wisdom (James 1:5) about the situation. Then, pray according to the Holy Spirit (Romans 8:26–27) and obey what He instructs you to say or do. (See the special feature at the end of this book for more about the Holy Spirit.)

Finally, but actually first and foremost in importance and priority, you must be born again to activate all the promises and provisions of God. (See John, chapter 3.)

Jesus Sets You Free!

Throughout this book, we've discussed how Satan came to steal, kill and destroy everything good in your life. The devil's deceptions, lies and attacks perpetrated against you and me are part of the curse that entered into the earth when Adam and Eve disobeyed God in the Garden. But, there's good news...

Jesus came to set people free from the curse—all those who would put their faith in what He did for them on the cross.

> Christ purchased our freedom [redeeming us] from the curse (doom) of the Law [and its condemnation] by [Himself] becoming a curse for us, for it is written [in the Scriptures], Cursed is everyone who hangs on a tree (is crucified); (Galatians 3:13 AMPC)

Know this, whether you are seeking freedom from a curse, sickness, poverty or a relationship gone bad, you can be confident in God's love. He has promised to never leave or forsake you. There is no enemy—Satan, a person, or any adversity—that can defeat you or stand in your way, "What shall we then say to these things? If God *be* for us, who (or what) *can* be against us?" (Romans 8:31 – parenthetical text mine).

Key Points

- Expect your healing, deliverance, family or financial breakthrough.
- Refuse to fear or compromise—God is faithful, and His Word is true.
- Refuse to blame others and walk in love. Love overcomes all evil.
- Forgiving others is critical if we want to receive answers to our prayers.
- Be sure that when your time on earth is ended, you are ready to spend eternity with Jesus.

Action Assignment:

Faith is your greatest weapon, but it only works through love. God is love, and there can be no power in our lives apart from His presence. Read James 4:7. Draw close to God, and the devil must flee! Also, read 1 Corinthians 13, the "love chapter." Ask yourself these questions: "Am I falling short in my love walk? What can I do today to show God's love to someone? Is there anyone I need to forgive from my heart for wronging me? **Say, "Father, I purpose** to take my eyes off my need, and I pray for (name) and their need. Show me if there's something I can do to help them. I forgive (name) from my heart and set them free from the wrong they did to me. I let it go, once and for all. I trust You to help me to love You with all my heart and to walk in love toward all people."

If you have not received Jesus Christ as your personal Savior and Lord, then you do not have God's promise of eternal life. Turn to the "Prayer for Salvation" in the prayer section at the back of this book. You will find instructions on how to make the best decision of your life and become part of the family of God!

God Has a Wonderful Gift for You

Believers who have been born again receive the Holy Spirit at the time of the new birth. However, as you see in the Bible, in Acts 1–2 and other scriptures, the disciples and believers received a second infilling of the Holy Spirit. This is the experience Jesus referred to when He said, "for John truly baptized with water, but you shall be baptized with the Holy Spirit not many days from now...But you shall receive power when the Holy Spirit has come upon you; and you shall be witnesses to Me in Jerusalem, and in all Judea and Samaria, and to the end of the earth" (Acts 1:5, 8 NKJV).

From my book, *The Baptism of the Holy Spirit*, I would like to share with you information about this wonderful gift of God, starting with a question that many ask...

Why do I really need the baptism of the Holy Spirit?

First of all, because Jesus said so! After Jesus had risen from the dead, He instructed His disciples, giving them the "great commission." Look in your Bible at Mark 16:15–18. Jesus commands His disciples (and us, His followers, today),

> [15] And He said to them, "Go into all the world and preach the gospel to every creature. [16] He who believes and is baptized will be saved; but he who does not believe

will be condemned. [17] And these signs will follow those who believe: In My name they will cast out demons; **they will speak with new tongues**; [18] they will take up serpents; and if they drink anything deadly, it will by no means hurt them; they will lay hands on the sick, and they will recover." (NKJV)

Purpose

Notice the results we should see and experience from believing in Jesus: To preach the gospel to every creature everywhere (verse 15), to free those who will believe from condemnation (verse 16), to bring salvation to those who will believe (verse 16), to bring deliverance to the oppressed (verse 17), and to bring healing to the sick (verse 18).

Protection

Those who are doing the work of God will be delivered from harm and the evil works of the enemy. (verse 18).

Power

The Holy Spirit-filled believer receives God's power to do the works of Jesus upon the earth. (verses 17–18) And these signs will follow...Casting out demons, healing the sick, and supernatural protection are possible only by the power of the Holy Spirit. Right in the middle of this scripture portion are the words, "they will speak with new tongues." This refers to those who have received the baptism of the Holy Spirit, as we will see later when we read about the Day of Pentecost.

In the book of Acts, where the Holy Spirit baptism first occurs, the disciples are waiting upon God for the power to witness and carry out Jesus' works now that He has ascended to heaven. It was necessary for them to receive this baptism before they went out to fulfill the "great commission" Jesus had given to them. Let's look at this important scripture portion again,

> "...Jesus instructed them, 'Don't leave Jerusalem, but wait here until you receive the gift I told you about, the gift the Father has promised. For John baptized you in water, but in a few days from now you will be baptized in the Holy Spirit... But I promise you this—the Holy Spirit will come upon you and you will be filled with power. And you will be my messengers to Jerusalem, throughout Judea, the distant provinces—even to the remotest places on earth!'" (Acts 1:4–5, 8 TPT)

You may already witness to people about Jesus, and that is commendable! However, after the baptism of the Holy Spirit, you will receive increased boldness and effectiveness in your witness. You will rely less on human intellect and more on the Holy Spirit, whose power will be residing more fully in you.

The first and most important reason for the baptism of the Holy Spirit is to enable the believer to effectively and powerfully share the gospel with the same signs

following as Jesus had in His ministry and as the apostles had in their ministries.

Have you ever prayed and wondered if you were praying in accordance with God's will? Or, have you struggled and just didn't know how to pray about a particular situation or need? We've all had that happen because prayer is not a mental or intellectual exercise. Prayer is connecting with God who is Spirit, so we know that prayer is a spiritual connection. Our human spirit, praying to God, needs to be empowered and enlightened by God's Spirit—the Holy Spirit—to be effective, and to produce results in line with God's plans and purposes. We do know much of God's will from studying His Word. However, we don't always know exactly which scriptures apply to the current concern, or the specific details of God's answer to our prayer. That's where the Holy Spirit helps us!

> Likewise the Spirit also helps in our weaknesses. For we do not know what we should pray for as we ought, and the Spirit Himself makes intercession for us with groanings which cannot be uttered. Now He who searches the hearts, knows what the mind of the Spirit is, because He makes intercession for the saints according to the will of God. (Romans 8:26–27 NKJV)

We can have peace knowing that our prayers will be answered because we are not praying out of our own understanding, preconceived ideas or fleshly desires, which may get in the way. The Holy Spirit knows the mind of God so He can help us in our weakness to pray in power and with confidence. Sometimes our understanding will be unfruitful—we won't have any idea what the Spirit is praying through us. "For if I pray in a tongue, my spirit prays, but my understanding is unfruitful" (1 Corinthians 14:14 NKJV). At other times, especially as we grow in praying in the Spirit, the Lord will give us a sense of what the Spirit is praying and sometimes even the interpretation of the prayer. "Therefore let him who speaks in a tongue pray that he may interpret" (1 Corinthians 14:13 NKJV). In this instance, Paul is talking about "tongues-speaking" in a church gathering; however, the instruction works the same in our private prayer times as well.

The second important reason for the baptism of the Holy Spirit is to enable the believer to pray according to God's will by the power of the Holy Spirit praying through him or her, while not being limited to their own understanding and desires.

Praying in the Holy Spirit (with the evidence of speaking in tongues) should be a vital component of your daily devotional time. There are no rules on how long you should pray in tongues, just let the Holy Spirit guide you. The more time you spend praying this way...the more you will desire to pray in the Spirit. You will draw closer to God than ever before; you will be more faithful and fruitful in serving Him. You will be stronger in overcoming weakness and temptation. You will have greater understanding of spiritual things, and greater victory in your life! Jude 20 in the *Modern English Version* tells us, "But you, beloved, build yourselves up in your most holy faith. Pray in the Holy Spirit."

Paul said to the believers in the Corinthian church,

> For he who speaks in an unknown tongue does not speak to men, but to God. For no one understands him, although in the spirit, he speaks mysteries. He who speaks in an unknown tongue edifies himself, but he who prophesies edifies the church. I desire that you all speak in tongues, but even more that you prophesy. For greater is he who prophesies than he who speaks in tongues, unless he interprets, so that the church may receive edification. (1 Corinthians 14:2, 4–5 MEV)

The third important reason for the baptism of the Holy Spirit is to edify the believer from the "inside-out." You will receive increased spiritual strength and victory, peace, understanding and comfort as a result of praying in the Holy Spirit.

Another question people—believers and unbelievers—often ask is this:

Wasn't this baptism only for the days of the Early Church?

No, no, no—a thousand times, no! How much more today, do these three reasons apply to the believers of Jesus Christ? We need just as much help from the Holy Spirit to effectively witness for Christ and to faithfully serve God. We certainly need His power to do the miraculous works that Jesus told us we would do. "Most assuredly, I say to you, he who believes in Me, the works that I do he will do also; and greater works than these he will do, because I go to My Father" (John 14:12 NKJV).

Greater material possessions and opportunities for temptation, as well as confusion and deception from the enemy, pull at us from every side. We certainly need the Holy Spirit's help—wisdom and discernment—in our prayer lives. And, to be built up, strengthened and edified, so that we can overcome sin and obstacles, and live a victorious Christian life.

As mentioned earlier, John the Baptist foretold that Jesus would baptize His followers with the Holy Spirit. "I (John, the Baptist) indeed baptized you with water, but He (Jesus) will baptize you with the Holy Spirit" (Mark 1:8 – parenthetical text mine). And Jesus Himself confirmed John's message in Acts 1:4–5, 8,

> And being assembled together with *them*, He commanded them not to depart from Jerusalem, but to wait for the Promise of the Father, "which," *He said*, "you have heard from Me; for John truly baptized with water, but you shall be baptized with the Holy Spirit not many days from now"..."but you shall receive power when the Holy Spirit has come upon you; and you shall be witnesses to Me in Jerusalem, and in Judea, and Samaria, and to the ends of the earth." (NKJV)

The Promise of the Father arrived gloriously on the Day of Pentecost. The event is described in Acts, chapter 2:

[1]When the Day of Pentecost had fully come, they were all with one accord in one place. [2]And suddenly, there came a sound from heaven, as of a rushing mighty wind, and it filled the whole house where they were sitting. [3]Then there appeared to them divided tongues, as of fire, and one sat upon each of them. [4]And they were all filled with the Holy Spirit and began to speak with other tongues, as the Spirit gave them utterance. [5]And there were dwelling in Jerusalem Jews, devout men, from every nation under heaven. [6]And when this sound occurred, the multitude came together, and were confused, because everyone heard them speak in his own language. [7]Then they were all amazed and marveled, saying to one another, "Look, are not all these who speak Galileans? [8]And how *is it that* we hear each in our own language in which we were born? [9]Parthians and Medes, and Elamites, those dwelling in Mesopotamia, Judea, and Cappadocia, Pontus and Asia, [10]Phrygia and Pamphylia, Egypt and parts of Libya adjoining Cyrene, visitors from Rome, both Jews and proselytes, [11]Cretans and Arabs—we hear them speaking in our

own tongues the wonderful works of God." [12]So they were all amazed and perplexed, saying to one another: "Whatever could this mean?" [13]Others mocking said, "They are full of new wine." [14]But Peter, standing up with the eleven raised his voice and said to them, "Men of Judea and all who dwell in Jerusalem, let this be known to you, and hear my words. [15]For these are not drunk, as you suppose, since it is *only* the third hour of the day. [16]But this is what was spoken by the prophet Joel: [17]'And it shall come to pass in the last days, says God, That I will pour out of My Spirit on all flesh; Your sons and your daughters shall prophesy, Your young men shall see visions, Your old men shall dream dreams, [18]And on My menservants and on My maidservants, I will pour out My Spirit in those days; And they shall prophesy.'" (Acts 2:1–18 NKJV)

The Day of Pentecost had come! The Day of God's Promise had come! However, many people didn't recognize the fulfillment of Joel's prophecy from the Old Testament that occurred on this historic day. They doubted and derided the believers. They just couldn't believe what they themselves couldn't understand with their human intellect.

So it is today, many people do not believe the miraculous and supernatural works of the Holy Spirit, even when they see them with their own eyes. Their hearts are hardened and their minds are blinded. They have been deceived by the teachings and vain philosophies of this world, and its ruler, the devil. But praise God, there are many that will listen and hear, and will be set free by the truth they receive.

As you continue to read Acts, chapter 2, you will see the new boldness with which Peter, the apostle, preached a powerful sermon to the crowd that had gathered to witness the great outpouring of the Holy Spirit. And, on that day alone, 3,000 souls were added to the community of believers. The apostles continued in the power of the Holy Spirit, preaching the good news about Jesus Christ; multitudes of people believed and were converted to Christ.

However, this wonderful experience of the baptism of the Holy Spirit was not reserved by God for the Jews alone. Much to their surprise, and the initial skepticism of the Hebrew people, God had a much bigger, broader plan in mind. If we are open to Him and yielded to His will, the Lord will always do "exceedingly abundantly above all that we could ask or think." (See Ephesians 3:20.)

Now, let's look at the following story about Cornelius, a Roman centurion, and other Gentiles who were also baptized with the Holy Spirit.

> While Peter was still speaking these words, the Holy Spirit fell upon all those who heard the word. And those of the circumcision (the Jews) who believed were astonished,

as many as came with Peter, because the gift of **the Holy Spirit had been poured out on the Gentiles also. For they heard them speak with tongues and magnify God...**" (Acts 10:44–46 NKJV – emphasis mine)

The bolded portion in the preceding scripture indicates that the evidence the Holy Spirit was poured out was that they spoke in "tongues." And so we see that not only Jews, but Gentiles, also received the Promise—it's for us today—Jew and Gentile alike, every ethnic group, rich and poor, educated and uneducated, male and female. The answer to this question is NO; this baptism wasn't just for the Early Church—the baptism of the Holy Spirit is for everyone, then and now, who will believe God and receive this gracious gift.

Do you have to speak with "tongues" to be baptized with the Holy Spirit?

As we have seen in Acts, chapters 2 and 10, when the believers were baptized with the Holy Spirit; this experience was accompanied by the evidence of speaking in other tongues. But, do you always have to speak with tongues if you have received this baptism? Paul obviously thought so. In 1 Corinthians, chapter 14, he told the church, "I wish you all spoke with tongues..." (verse 5), and "I thank my God I speak with tongues more than you all..." (verse 18).

Let's look at another instance where the evidence of the Holy Spirit baptism included speaking with tongues:

And it happened while Apollos was at
Corinth, that Paul, having passed through
the upper regions, came to Ephesus. And
finding some disciples, he said to them,
'Did you receive the Holy Spirit when you
believed?' So they said to him, 'We have
not so much as heard whether there is a
Holy Spirit.' And he said to them, 'Into
what then were you baptized?' So they
said, 'Into John's baptism.' Then Paul said,
'John indeed baptized with a baptism of
repentance, saying to the people that they
should believe on Him who would come
after him, that is, on Christ Jesus.' When
they heard *this*, they were baptized in the
name of the Lord Jesus. And when Paul laid
hands on them, the Holy Spirit came upon
them, and they spake with tongues and
prophesied." (Acts 19:1–6 NKJV)

It appears from Scripture that when people were
baptized with the Holy Spirit, they also spoke in a tongue
they had not formerly known. **It was a prayer language
received not as a result of study and learning, but as a
gift from God.**

I do not believe we can rigidly, legalistically, declare
that a person absolutely cannot be baptized with the Holy
Spirit if they don't speak with tongues. But, with all the
benefits you receive from this gift, why would you want
to miss it? Why would you say, "No" to God, "I don't

162

want this beautiful, powerful, joyful gift You are offering to me."?

Personally, I thank God for this supernatural ability to speak "in mysteries" directly to Him, and to see the revelation and results that come from not being limited by my own natural language and understanding. I thank God for the joy, peace and strength that come from a time of prayer "with other tongues." I thank God that as I intercede in my Holy Spirit prayer language He is doing great works for people, and in situations, I don't know anything about. Praise God for using us in this wonderful way as instruments in His plan for others. What an awesome privilege!

Of course, like with prayer in your own native language, you can simply be mouthing words without any real heart commitment. But, if you love the Lord and are truly seeking Him, He will not disappoint you. As you speak with other tongues, you will grow in knowledge, and experience a deeper walk with Jesus through the Holy Spirit. "For the Lord is the Spirit, and wherever the Spirit of the Lord is, there is freedom" (2 Corinthians 3:17 NLT).

Why isn't some of today's "tongues-speaking" an actual known language according to linguistic experts?

This is another objection brought up by critics of the baptism of the Holy Spirit. They point to Acts, chapter 2, noting that the baptized believers were speaking in actual languages, not just in what today sounds like gibberish. This is true. At the first outpouring of the Holy Spirit, the apostles and other believers spoke in a variety of languages that were known and understood by the crowd of onlookers, though these languages were not known or understood by the apostles and believers speaking them. This experience was also accompanied by "a sound from heaven as of a rushing mighty wind" and "divided tongues, as of fire, and one sat upon each of them" (see verses 2–3). These signs were not recorded in later instances, nor was there any mention later of the tongues" being actual known languages.

"Tongues-speaking" is sometimes a known language (though not to the believer speaking it) and sometimes not a known language. Linguistic experts have studied and documented many languages, but have not exhausted every language upon the face of the earth. A language which nobody recognizes may nevertheless be a valid language somewhere. At certain times believers have spoken "with tongues"; others have heard them and verified that the believers were actually speaking in the hearers' native tongue. God uses these situations as signs to the hearer, usually an unbeliever, to share and validate the gospel.

There are actually three kinds of tongues, which we'll discuss later. Note also, that tongues may sound different in individual persons, just as natural languages do.

Don't miss this wonderful experience of "speaking with other tongues" that accompanies the baptism of the Holy Spirit. It's not scary, or contrary to Scripture, and it is for TODAY! Put away preconceived notions; seek Jesus sincerely in faith, as a little child, for Jesus is the Holy Spirit Baptizer!

Another question, or fear, that causes people to avoid or reject receiving this wonderful gift from God is this:

What if I get the wrong thing—like some kind of demonic manifestation or false tongue?

There is another common fear among Christians who love the Lord and want all of His will for them, but nevertheless shy away from the baptism of the Holy Spirit. It is the concern that they may somehow receive a false or demonic manifestation or counterfeit tongue rather than the real thing. My brother and my sister, let me assure you—this is not possible.

When you believed unto salvation, were you afraid of getting the wrong "Jesus?" And you were much less knowledgeable about the things of God then than you are now. If you trusted Jesus for salvation, trust Him now for the baptism of the Holy Spirit, for Jesus is the One who baptizes with the Holy Spirit or Holy Ghost as the *King James Version* reads, "I indeed have baptized you with water: but he shall baptize you with the Holy Ghost" (Mark 1:8).

God loves you. You are His child. Will the Father trick His beloved child? Look at the following portion of Scripture in Luke 11:9–13:

> So I say to you, Ask *and* keep on asking and it shall be given you; seek *and* keep on seeking and you shall find; knock *and* keep on knocking and the door shall be opened to you. For everyone who asks *and* keeps on asking receives; and he who seeks *and* keeps on seeking finds; and to him who knocks *and* keeps on knocking, the door shall be opened. What father among you,

> if his son asks for *a loaf of bread, will give
> him a stone; or if he asks for* a fish, will
> instead of a fish give him a serpent? Or if he
> asks for an egg, will give him a scorpion? If
> you then, evil as you are, know how to give
> good gifts [gifts that are to their advantage]
> to your children, how much more will your
> heavenly Father give the Holy Spirit to
> those who ask *and* continue to ask Him!
> (AMPC)

If you are born again, your Father is God, and your Lord is Jesus Christ. And it is the same Holy Spirit Who came to dwell in you when you were born again, Who now desires to gloriously fill you fully with Himself, and to commune with you in a greater measure. Paul ends his letter to the Corinthian church with, "The grace (favor and spiritual blessing) of the Lord Jesus Christ and the love of God and the presence *and* fellowship (the communion and sharing together, and participation) in the Holy Spirit be with you all. *Amen (so be it)...*" (2 Corinthians 13:14 AMPC). Don't grieve or quench the Holy Spirit—accept His call for a deeper relationship with you, and walk with Him. You have nothing to fear, nothing to lose, and everything to gain!

Don't let fear rob you of a deeper walk with Jesus and His Holy Spirit. God loves you—you are His child. You trusted Jesus for salvation; now trust Him for the baptism of the Holy Spirit, for Jesus is the Holy Spirit Baptizer!

Why do some people who claim to have this experience still sin? That's a good question. The Bible teaches the result of accepting Jesus Christ as Savior: "Therefore, if anyone is in Christ, he is a new creation; old things have passed away; behold, all things have become new" (2 Corinthians 5:17 NKJV). When you are saved, Jesus becomes your Lord and you are no longer ruled by Satan, but by the Son of God. Jesus now lives in you!

Being born again initiates a process of learning about God, His ways and His will. One by one, you hand over habits and parts of your life and your heart to the Lordship of Jesus Christ. You become no longer conformed to this world, but transformed by the renewing of your mind according to the Word of God. (See Romans 12:2.) Sanctification is a process. And, just as a toddler trips and falls as he is learning, so do baby Christians.

Being filled with the Holy Spirit is also a process. There is the initial infilling, which Jesus referred to as the baptism of the Holy Spirit. As a result, you will receive the new prayer language of "other tongues," and notice dramatic changes in your spiritual understanding, strength and boldness for witnessing and service. But, just as you grow in grace and maturity as a new Christian by spending time in God's Word and prayer; you must continuously yield to the Holy Spirit's infilling through praying in the Spirit and obedience to His voice and to the Word of God.

The Holy Spirit is just what His Name implies—holy. He can be quenched or grieved by sin and disobedience. Your body is the temple of the Holy Spirit; therefore glorify

God in your body and in your spirit. (See 1 Corinthians 6:19–20.)

The Voice of the Holy Spirit Is Gentle, as He Is Gentle

You must be listening and seeking the Lord in order to hear His voice. He will not force Himself on you, nor will He make you follow His leading. Though we are saved and filled with the Holy Spirit, we still have a free will and the power to make choices—right or wrong.

When you have received the baptism of the Holy Spirit, you must be careful to treat the Holy Spirit with respect just as you would Jesus and the Father. Sin, self-will, and a desire for the things of the flesh and of the world are some of the reasons that cause believers to fall away from the Lord and refuse the communion of His Spirit. Neglect or indifference to the things of God, or just plain busyness, will also hinder our relationship with the Holy Spirit and our sensitivity to hearing His voice.

The Baptism of the Holy Spirit Strengthens Us and Helps Us to Overcome Temptation

In addition to overcoming temptation, we receive greater power to be more effective witnesses for Christ and to fulfill the plan of God for our lives. But, with every blessing and gift from God comes responsibility. We must be faithful to nurture this gift through exercising our prayer language as well as in submission and obedience to the Lord. We must be careful not to resist or block out the voice of the Holy Spirit. He has been given to us for our good!

Some who have been baptized with the Holy Spirit are content to have a very minimal experience with Him. Once having received the initial baptism, they do not grow further or deeper—just as some who are born again do not grow, but rather remain carnal Christians. This is a sad, ineffective Christian existence. Those who choose this way miss many blessings, and later on also, they will miss the rewards that are stored up in heaven for those who are faithful.

It is this type of Christian, though having received the baptism of the Holy Spirit and even speaking in tongues, who walks that uneven and shaky line, trying to hold on to both the things of God and the things of this world. It is this person, who is most likely to indulge in sin while still speaking in tongues.

Don't Let the Failures of Another Steal God's Precious Gift, the Baptism of the Holy Spirit, from You

But understand this, that in the last days will come (set in) perilous times of great stress *and* trouble [hard to deal with and hard to bear]. For people will be lovers of self *and* [utterly] self-centered, lovers of money *and* aroused by an inordinate [greedy] desire for wealth, proud *and* arrogant *and* contemptuous boasters. They will be abusive (blasphemous, scoffing), disobedient to parents, ungrateful, unholy *and* profane. [They will be] without natural [human] affection (callous and inhuman), relentless (admitting of no truce or appeasement); [they will be] slanderers (false accusers, troublemakers), intemperate *and* loose in morals *and* conduct, uncontrolled *and* fierce, haters of good. [They will be] treacherous [betrayers], rash, [and] inflated with self-conceit. [They will be] lovers of sensual pleasures *and* vain amusements more than *and* rather than lovers of God. For [although] they hold a form of piety (true religion), they deny *and* reject *and* are strangers to the power of it [their conduct belies the genuineness of their profession]. Avoid [all] such people [turn away from them]. (2 Timothy 3:1–5 AMPC)

Don't be discouraged by those, who have received the Holy Spirit baptism, yet still walk in sin. We are not to judge them, but to be accountable to God for our own obedience and acceptance of His will.

Didn't Paul tell the Corinthian church not to speak in tongues?

Not exactly. Let's look at chapter 14 in the book of 1st Corinthians,

I thank God that I speak in [strange] tongues (languages) more than any of you *or* all of you put together; Nevertheless, **in public worship**, I would rather say five words with my understanding *and* intelligently in order to instruct others, than ten thousand words in a [strange] tongue (language).

Brethren, do not be children [immature] in your thinking; continue to be babes in [matters of] evil, but in your minds be mature [men]. It is written in the Law, By men of strange languages *and* by the lips of foreigners will I speak to this people, and not even then will they listen to Me, says the Lord. Thus [unknown] tongues are meant for a [supernatural] sign, not for believers but for unbelievers [on the point of believing], while prophecy (inspired preaching and teaching, interpreting the divine will and purpose) is not for unbelievers [on the point of believing] but for believers. Therefore, if the whole church assembles and all of you speak in [unknown] tongues, and the ungifted *and* uninitiated or unbelievers come in, will they not say that you are demented? But if all prophesy [giving inspired testimony and interpreting the divine will and purpose] and an unbeliever or untaught outsider comes in, he is told of his sin *and* reproved *and* convicted *and* convinced by all, and his defects *and* needs are examined (estimated, determined) *and* he is called to account by all, The secrets of his heart are laid bare; and so, falling on

[his] face, he will worship God, declaring that God is among you in very truth. What then, brethren, is [the right course]? When you meet together, each one has a hymn, a teaching, a disclosure of special knowledge *or* information, an utterance in a [strange] tongue, or an interpretation of it. [But] let everything be constructive *and* edifying *and* for the good of all. If some speak in a [strange] tongue, let the number be limited to two or at the most three, and each one [taking his] turn, and let one interpret *and* explain [what is said]. But if there is no one to do the interpreting, let each of them keep still in church and talk to himself and to God. So let two or three prophets speak [those inspired to preach or teach], while the rest pay attention *and* weigh *and* discern what is said. But if an inspired revelation comes to another who is sitting by, then let the first one be silent. For in this way you can give testimony [prophesying and thus interpreting the divine will and purpose] one by one, so that all may be instructed and all may be stimulated *and* encouraged; For the spirits of the prophets (the speakers in tongues) are under the speaker's control [and subject to being silenced as may be necessary], For He [Who is the source of their prophesying] is not a God of confusion

and disorder but of peace *and* order...If anyone thinks *and* claims that he is a prophet [filled with and governed by the Holy Spirit of God and inspired to interpret the divine will and purpose in preaching or teaching] or has any other spiritual endowment, let him understand (recognize and acknowledge) that what I am writing to you is a command of the Lord. But if anyone disregards *or* does not recognize [that it is a command of the Lord], he is disregarded *and* not recognized [he is one whom God knows not]. So [to conclude], my brethren, earnestly desire *and* set your hearts on prophesying (on being inspired to preach and teach and to interpret God's will and purpose), and do not forbid *or* hinder speaking in [unknown] tongues. (1 Corinthians 14:18–39 AMPC – emphasis mine)

Here, Paul is talking about **public** "tongues-speaking" that occurs during a church service.

Three Types of Tongues

Sometimes, people get confused about speaking in tongues because there are actually three different types of tongues-speaking shown in the New Testament: (1) An actual language as shown in Acts, chapter 2, (2) a believer's personal prayer language as described previously, and (3) public tongues used to prophesy in a church service for edification of believers and as a sign to unbelievers. It is a gift of the Holy Spirit. (See 1 Corinthians, chapter 12.)

The Corinthian church was very "spiritual." They desired to operate in the gifts of the Holy Spirit. But evidently, their speaking in (public) tongues got out of hand. It appears that people were speaking with tongues at the same time, and there wasn't always an interpreter present. Therefore, they were out of order! This is what Paul was correcting, not the fact that they spoke with tongues, since in verse 39, we read, "...do not forbid to speak with tongues." Paul also encouraged the believers to speak in tongues, saying: "I thank my God I speak with tongues more than you all..." (verse 18).

Tongues as a Gift of the Holy Spirit

Public tongues are used to prophesy in a church service for the edification of believers and as a sign to unbelievers. This type of tongues is a gift of the Holy Spirit, as shown in 1 Corinthians 12:4–11,

> Now there are distinctive varieties *and* distributions of endowments (gifts, extraordinary powers distinguishing certain Christians, due to the power of divine grace operating in their souls by the Holy Spirit) and they vary, but the [Holy] Spirit remains the same. And there are distinctive varieties of service *and* ministration, but it is the same Lord [Who is served]. And there are distinctive varieties of operation [of working

to accomplish things], but it is the same God Who inspires *and* energizes them all in all. But to each one is given the manifestation of the [Holy] Spirit [the evidence, the spiritual illumination of the Spirit] for good *and* profit. To one is given in *and* through the [Holy] Spirit [the power to speak] a message of wisdom, and to another [the power to express] a word of knowledge *and* understanding according to the same [Holy] Spirit; To another [wonder-working] faith by the same [Holy] Spirit, to another the extraordinary powers of healing by the one Spirit; To another the working of miracles, to another prophetic insight (the gift of interpreting the divine will and purpose); to another the ability to discern *and* distinguish between [the utterances of true] spirits [and false ones], to another various kinds of [unknown] tongues, to another the ability to interpret [such] tongues. All these [gifts, achievements, abilities] are inspired *and* brought to pass by one and the same [Holy] Spirit, Who apportions to each person individually [exactly] as He chooses. (AMPC)

One objection you'll hear from believers trying to substantiate their rejection of the baptism of the Holy Spirit goes along these lines, "In the Bible it says that not all believers speak in tongues. The Holy Spirit distributes gifts as He wills." The confusion comes in because the believer who uses this excuse doesn't realize that there are different types of tongues. And the tongues, to which he is referring, is not the prayer language that Paul says is for every believer, but rather one of the gifts of the Holy Spirit mentioned in chapter 12 of 1st Corinthians.

Public Versus Private Tongues

Yes, this type of public tongues is only given as the Holy Spirit wills and as sought after by the believer. This is the one that causes confusion and criticism when there is no one present in the church service to interpret. The "tongues," which are either an actual native language or a believer's individual prayer language, are meant for every believer. We know this because Jesus told His followers to wait in Jerusalem until after the Promise of the Father had come. (See Acts, chapters 1 and 2.)

The Bible describes clearly the reasons tongues have been given as a gift of the Holy Spirit: as a sign to the unbeliever and for edification of the church. Paul urges believers to prophesy so that the whole church may be edified (see 1 Corinthians 14); however, he also informs the believers that when there are tongues along with interpretation of tongues; this is equal to prophecy in value for edification of the church.

The baptism of the Holy Spirit "tongues" is a personal prayer language God has given to believers to communicate directly with Him. This is different from the public display of tongues that is a gift of the Holy Spirit to the Church.

The personal prayer language of a believer is quite different than the public gift as we have already seen. Here we see something interesting. Sandwiched between 1 Corinthians 12 and 14, is the "love chapter," chapter 13. The first sentence refers to "tongues of angels." "Though I speak with the tongues of men and of angels, but have not love, I have become sounding brass or a clanging cymbal" (verse 1 NKJV). This doesn't provide much information, but it does appear to refer to a heavenly language, perhaps related to the tongues given to the believer as evidence of the baptism of the Holy Spirit. Here too, the angelic tongue is different from the language of men.

> That is what is meant by the Scriptures which say that no mere man has ever seen, heard, or even imagined what wonderful things God has ready for those who love the Lord. But we know about these things because God has sent his Spirit to tell us, and his Spirit searches out and shows us all of God's deepest secrets. No one can really know what anyone else is thinking or what he is really like except that person himself. And no one can know God's thoughts except God's own Spirit. And God has actually given us his Spirit (not the world's spirit) to tell us about the wonderful free gifts of grace and blessing that God has given us. (1 Corinthians 2:9–12 TLB)

177

When we pray in tongues, we are praying the mind and things of God which only the Holy Spirit knows. The baptism of the Holy Spirit will revitalize your prayer life, making it more rewarding and productive, as well as your praise and worship—You can sing in tongues, too! (See again 1 Corinthians, chapter 14.)

As a born-again believer, the Holy Spirit already dwells in you. But the word, "baptism" means to be immersed. You will be filled full of the Holy Spirit and the power of God for the purposes we've already covered.

Being filled with the Holy Spirit is not just a one-time event though. It is important to continue seeking God for a fresh infilling of His Holy Spirit. This will happen as you spend time with the Holy Spirit, in God's Word, and in a growing relationship with Jesus Christ. Even seasoned believers should seek God for a fresh touch from the Holy Spirit.

The Holy Spirit baptism helps us to discern God's will. As we pray in the Spirit, we are actually praying God's will and plan from the spiritual realm into the natural realm. This Holy Spirit prayer accomplishes these three things: (1) You receive God's wisdom, knowledge and discernment, (2) Obstacles are removed and doors open, and (3) God's plan is birthed to accomplish His will, provision and blessings for the divine assignment He's given you.

In your prayer time, it's a good idea to begin praying in tongues first as the Holy Spirit leads. Then following this, when you pray in your native language, you can be assured that you are still being led by the Holy Spirit. Sometimes,

He will give you the interpretation of what you prayed in tongues—this is really exciting! Other times, you will be praying merely according to your human understanding, but this is good, because the Father wants you to communicate from your heart to Him, too. He cares about the thoughts, feelings and needs you share with Him. But just remember, there is no set formula. You need to give your attention to the Holy Spirit, and He will lead you.

Scriptural Methods for Receiving the Baptism of the Holy Spirit

(1) **Sovereign Move of God** (see Acts, chapter 2): Initial outpouring of the Holy Spirit as foretold by the prophet Joel on the Day of Pentecost. Christ, too, had told them about this event—the baptism of the Holy Spirit. This manifestation included a heavenly sound as of a rushing mighty wind, and divided tongues of fire. They also spoke in actual languages, which they did not previously know or learn. People often ask why these "signs" don't accompany today's baptism of the Holy Spirit experiences. This is because the Holy Spirit has already been given on the Day of Pentecost.

We don't have to wait any longer on God for His Promise—All we have to do now is to personally ask Him for the baptism of the Holy Spirit, just as you asked Jesus to come into your heart and life. As for the language question, there have been documented and witnessed cases where a believer will be speaking in an unknown (to him or her) tongue, and the person hearing it will confirm that it is an actual language, usually their native tongue. You will note also, that in other biblical accounts where people were baptized with the Holy Spirit, there was no indication that the same manifestations as on the Day of Pentecost occurred.

(2) **Preaching the Word of God** (see Acts, chapter 10): As Peter preached Jesus Christ to the household of Cornelius, the Holy Spirit fell on all those who heard the Word. None of them—the Jews or the Gentiles—were expecting or seeking that experience. But God knows the hearts of people and their readiness to receive more from Him.

(3) **Laying On of Hands** (see Acts 19:1–6): In Ephesus, Paul inquired of some disciples if they had received the Holy Spirit. After he had explained more to them about the baptism of the Holy Spirit, Paul laid hands on the disciples. The Holy Spirit came upon them, and they spoke with tongues and prophesied.

How to Receive the Baptism of the Holy Spirit

There are three steps to receiving the baptism of the Holy Spirit:

(1) Know what God's Word, the Bible, says about this wonderful gift from God. That has been the purpose of this special study to provide scriptural knowledge about the baptism of the Holy Spirit. Please go through any portions of it again, or study additional scriptures in the Bible, if you are unsure of your understanding on this subject.

(2) Spend some time in praise and worship unto the Lord. God inhabits our praises. In Acts, chapter 2, it says that they were all in one accord. Make sure there is no strife in your life or unforgiveness in your heart toward

anyone. Repent of any known sin according to 1 John 1:9: "If we confess our sins, He is faithful and just to forgive us our sins and to cleanse us from all unrighteousness." If you have been putting other things or people before God, this is a good time to repent of that also and ask Him to renew your first love for the Lord Jesus Christ.

(3) Ask God by faith for the baptism of the Holy Spirit. "But without faith *it is* impossible to please *Him*, for he who comes to God must believe that He is, and *that* He is a rewarder of those who diligently seek Him." (Hebrews 11:6 NKJV)

Put it in your own words, or pray something like this:

"Dear God,

I am a born-again believer. I am Your child. I understand that You love me and desire to fill me with Your Holy Spirit. I believe Your Word is true. Your Word says that if I ask, and believe, I will receive the Holy Spirit. So, in the Name of Jesus Christ, my Lord, I am asking You to fill me to overflowing with Your Holy Spirit.

"Jesus, according to Your Word, You are the One who baptizes with the Holy Spirit, so I am asking You now to baptize me with the Holy Spirit. I thank You for the baptism of the Holy Spirit which I believe I have received. I also believe, by faith, that I will speak in tongues now as the Spirit gives me utterance. Amen"

After you have prayed and asked God to fill you with the Holy Spirit:

Begin to speak as the Holy Spirit gives you utterance.

Open your mouth and say whatever words are in your heart or come to mind no matter how silly or strange they may sound to you. They will be from the Holy Spirit.

Even if there is only one syllable, speak it out again and again. You will be praising and praying to God in your new prayer language! Just as a baby, or young child, learns new words, your Spirit "vocabulary" will increase. Don't worry if you only have a few words, or even just one word to start. Sometimes, a whole flood of words will come. Don't hold back, but speak them out boldly. Whichever way it happens, it's real!

The important thing is to keep praying in tongues every day. Don't let doubt or fear rise up and steal the wonderful gift you have received. Keep exercising this gift of tongues, and rejoice in your new relationship with the Holy Spirit. Commune with Him daily for He is the Spirit of the Lord and will abide with you forever!

Remember, the baptism of the Holy Spirit, along with the outward evidence of speaking in tongues, is just the beginning. You will begin to experience a closer relationship with the Lord and more power to witness and serve Him. You will receive greater revelation and understanding of spiritual things. Purposefully yield each day to the Holy Spirit. Obey God's Word and repent of any sin as soon as you become aware of it. Ask God to fill you afresh and anew each day with His Spirit, His wisdom, power and love.

Congratulations as you embark on this great new adventure with the awesome Holy Spirit of God!

NOTE: *If you haven't received the manifestation of speaking in tongues, or have other questions, seek out a church leader or believer who has experienced the baptism of the Holy Spirit. Ask them to lay hands on you and help you to receive the Holy Spirit. Above all, don't give up. Keep seeking Jesus and He will not disappoint you. He is the Holy Spirit Baptizer.*

Appendices

Healings, Deliverances and Miracles of Jesus

Man with leprosy	Matthew 8:1–4, Mark 1:40–45, Luke 5:12–15
Centurion's servant	Matthew 8:5–13, Luke 7:1–10
Peter's mother–in–law	Matthew 8:14–15, Mark 1:29–31, Luke 4:38–39
Casting out demons	Matthew 8:28–34, Mark 5:1–20, Luke 8:26–39
Paralyzed man	Matthew 9:1–8, Mark 2, 1–12, Luke 5:17–26
Woman with issue of blood	Matthew 9:20–22, Mark 5:25–34, Luke 8:43–48,
Two blind men	Matthew 9:27–31
Mute, demon-possessed man	Matthew 9:32–33, Luke 11:14
Man with shriveled hand	Matthew 12:9–13, Mark 3:1–5, Luke 6:6–10
Blind, mute, possessed man	Matthew 12:22–23
Canaanite woman's daughter	Matthew 15:21–28, Mark 7:24–30
Boy with a demon	Matthew 17:14–21, Mark 9:14–29, Luke 9:37–42
Blind Bartimaeus	Matthew 20:29–34, Mark 10:46–52, Luke 18:35–43
Deaf mute	Mark 7:31–37
Possessed man in Synagogue	Mark 1:21–28, Luke 4:31–37
Blind man at Bethsaida	Mark 8:22–26
Crippled woman	Luke 13:10–17
Man with dropsy	Luke 14:1–4
Ten lepers	Luke 17:11–19
High Priest's servant	Luke 22:49–51
Official's son	John 4:46–54
Sick man at Pool of Bethesda	John 5:1–15
Man born blind	John 9:1–41
Jairus' daughter	Matthew 9:18–19, 23–26, Mark 5:21–24, 35–43, Luke 8:40–42, 49–56
Widow's son	Luke 7:11–17
Lazarus	John 11:1–44

Calming the storm	Matthew 8:23–27, Mark 4:35–41, Luke 8:22–25
Feeding the 5,000	Matthew 14:13–21, Mark 6:32–44, Luke 9:10–17, John 6:1–13
Walking on water	Matthew 14:22–33, Mark 6:45–51, John 6:16–21
Feeding the 4,000	Matthew 15:29–38, Mark 8:1–9
Coin in fish's mouth	Matthew 17:24–27
Fig tree withered at roots	Matthew 21:18–22, Mark 11:12–14, 20–25
Large catch of fish	Luke 5:4–11
Water turned to wine	John 2:1–11
Another large catch of fish	John 21:1–11

PRAYERS FOR YOU

Prayer for Salvation

"For God so loved the world that He gave His only begotten Son, that whoever believes in Him should not perish, but have everlasting life" (John 3:16 NKJV).

"For all have sinned and fall short of the glory of God" (Romans 3:23 NKJV). God is a holy God, and we cannot stand before Him, nor enter into heaven, in our sin.

But God has made a way. He sent His own Son, Jesus Christ, to be crucified on a cross for our sins. Jesus took the punishment we deserved upon Himself so that we could be made right with God. "For He (God) made Him (Jesus Christ) who knew no sin *to be* sin for us, that we might become the righteousness of God in Him" (2 Corinthians 5:21 NKJV). But, it didn't end there. God raised Jesus up from the grave, and He is alive today, sitting at the right hand of God in heaven!

How do you receive this wonderful gift of salvation through Jesus Christ?
"...If you confess with your mouth the Lord Jesus and believe in your heart that God has raised Him from the dead, you will be saved. For with the heart one believes unto righteousness, and with the mouth confession is made unto salvation" (Romans 10:9–10 NKJV).

If you sincerely believe Jesus is the Son of God, all you need to do is ask Him to be your personal Savior and Lord. You can pray something like this:

"Dear God,

I believe that Jesus Christ is Your Son, and that He died on the cross to pay the price for my sins. I also believe that You raised Him from the dead that I might have new life in Him. I repent of my sins and ask You to forgive me. Jesus, come into my heart; be my Savior and Lord. Help me to live for You and to fulfill the wonderful plan God has for my life. Thank you, Lord, for saving me. I am a born-again child of God. Amen."

Welcome to the family of God, brother or sister! Get into a Bible-believing church, and tell someone about your new Friend, Jesus. Read the Bible yourself and talk to God in prayer every day. Now, you have become eligible to receive the baptism of the Holy Spirit—an awesome and precious gift from God to you!

Prayer for Holy Spirit Baptism

(See previous instructions preceding this section of prayers.)

Healing

Dear God, I thank You that Jesus bore my sin, sickness, weakness and pain on the cross at Calvary. I thank You that He was wounded for my transgressions and bruised for my iniquities. I thank You that the chastisement needed to obtain my peace was laid upon Jesus, and by His stripes I am healed from (name your symptoms or the doctor's diagnosis).

I speak now to every sickness and disease, "You have no right to exist in my body. Go now, in Jesus' Name! Every pain, every symptom, every fear and doubt, I command you to leave my presence now.

I speak the blood of Jesus over my mind, emotions and body, from the top of my head to the soles of my feet. I declare that every body part—every organ, bone, muscle, joint, tissue, cell (name your affected body part)—functions in the perfection to which God created it for I am fearfully and wonderfully made. I declare God's healing power over every bodily system—my respiratory, circulatory, skeletal, digestive (name your affected bodily system or function)—it is healed completely, in Jesus' Name.

I am healed, whole and strong in the Lord and in the power of His might. Amen!

Deliverance

Father, I praise You that in Christ Jesus, You have given me power and authority over all the power of the enemy. In Jesus' Name, I rebuke every foul, tormenting spirit that is oppressing me, my mind and emotions. I cast out the spirit of (name whatever is coming against you: infirmity, addiction, anger, rejection, confusion, strife, depression, cancer, diabetes, blindness, deafness, witchcraft, inability to sleep, etc.) by the power and authority Christ has given to me.

I take authority over every demonic spirit, infirmity, pain, disease (name it) now and command you to loose your hold on me (or name of another). I command you to go. You will not afflict or harass me (or them) any longer. I (or they) have been set free, for whom the Son sets free is free indeed. In Jesus' Name, Amen!

Family

Dear God, thank you for my family (name each member you want to pray for). I declare now that they are saved and walking in the Spirit of God. They are new creations in Christ Jesus and set free from sin and every evil work of the devil.

I thank You that you have a good plan for each of them, and I call your plans forth now into their lives. I pray that they grow in grace, forgiveness, and in the knowledge of God and His will.

I rebuke any strife, jealousy, anger, deception or confusion from operating in our house. We live by the fruit of the Holy Spirit: love, joy, peace, patience, goodness, kindness, faithfulness, gentleness and self-control.

I forgive (names) for (name the wrong they committed against you) by faith and will remember it no more just as God has forgiven me (us) and remembers my (our) sins no more.

Thank you, Jesus, that You are Lord over my house. We give no place to the devil. We reject his lies and interference in our home. We love and support each other, and even when we disagree, we do so respectfully and with humility. Our home is Christ-centered and God-blessed! In Jesus' Name, Amen!

Prosperity

Through Jesus Christ, I am the seed of Abraham and have received all the promises and blessings God gave to Abraham. I prosper in my soul, my health and in my finances. Thank you that You have given me all that is necessary to fulfill every obligation and need, and to have enough left over to give to the work of God and to help others. I thank You, Father, for blessing the work of my hands and for multiplying back to me every seed I sow.

As I tithe into the kingdom of God, I believe according to Your Word the windows of heaven are open over my family and me and You are pouring out a blessing that is so abundant we can hardly contain it. I thank You also for Your promise to rebuke the devourer when I tithe and that he will not touch me, my family, our home, finances or possessions, or anything else that is of concern to us.

Thank you for wisdom, revelation knowledge and understanding where my finances are concerned. I receive creative ideas, concepts and insights from heaven, and I declare that Jesus is Lord over my finances and my business (or job). I will meditate in God's Word daily and have good success. In Jesus' Name, Amen.

General

Dear God, I thank You for saving me, healing me, protecting and providing for all of my needs. You do exceedingly abundantly above all that I could ask or think.

Thank you for watching over my family and me and all that is ours. I thank You that Your plans for us are good and not evil; Your plans prosper and do not harm us. Your plans are filled with hope and a good future.

I ask for wisdom for this day and for every matter that arises. I thank You that I am always in the right place at the right time with the right people doing the right thing and that You order my steps according to Your perfect will.

I receive Your favor and direction concerning my family, finances, business or job, and relationships. Help me to be faithful to serve You and others, and to take my place in Your divine plan. In Jesus' Name, Amen.

THE ANSWER BOOK for Troubled Times

by Holly Lewerenz

This book answers the hard questions that people are asking today—without political bias or blame games!

Economic upheaval, political discord, and uncertain future hovers over America and the world like a dark and ominous cloud. . .bringing fear, confusion and distrust. Many are asking, "What's going to happen to me?" Few stop to think that behind the stage of stinging words and spontaneous outbursts of rage, there is a dynamic word called. . .**DESTINY!**

Have you ever asked yourself these questions:

- ▶ What is the purpose of all that is going on around me?
- ▶ Where do I fit in? Is there any real purpose for my life?
- ▶ Am I just spinning my wheels? Am I just marking time?

THE ANSWER BOOK for Troubled Times is a book for everybody—Americans, other world nations, Israelis, Muslims, and Christians! No matter what your spiritual beliefs, your political beliefs or your personal beliefs, this informative book will speak to you! THE ANSWER BOOK for Troubled Times will answer the questions on your heart and mind about the critical times we are living in:

- Why these are not just random circumstances, but carefully laid plans of greedy men, lusting for power, who desire to take over the world
- How the current financial crisis and other events precede the coming one-world currency and global government
- Discover the rise of the antichrist and false prophet who will rule the world until they meet their devastating demise
- Why a tiny country like Israel draws such huge interest and conflict
- Two kinds of Muslims—what are their roles in these end-time days?
- How the Church can bring relief and hope to a hurting world
- How you can live supernaturally safe with peace that overrides any attack against you or your family
- What is the answer for America to stand strong and regain her respected place in the world?

Order Now on Amazon.com, BarnesandNoble.com, Google Play and other secure, ecommerce websites. If you would like more information, please feel free to visit our website at HealingforAmerica.com or call us at (817) 285-0058.